Teaching
Narrative Writing

The Tools That Work for Every Student

BY LOLA M. SCHAEFER

SCHOLASTIC
PROFESSIONAL BOOKS

NEW YORK • TORONTO • LONDON • AUCKLAND • SYDNEY
MEXICO CITY • NEW DELHI • HONG KONG

*To all my students, past and present, who graciously included me
as a fellow writer—may you continue to share the stories in your hearts.*

*Thank you to the members of my readers/writers group:
Laura, Erica, Sarah, Lauren, Lindie, Marie, and Amanda.*

*A special thank you to Dr. Maxine Huffman, who ignited and encouraged
the true learner and teacher in me many years ago.*

ACKNOWLEDGMENTS

Teachers and writers do not work alone. Our work is refined only through the questions, dialogue, and experimentation we share with others. Fortunately, I am surrounded by outstanding professionals, both teachers and students, who include me in their thoughtful practice. It is through these collaborations that I continue to grow and gain new insight.

Thank you to all the students who allowed me to publish their stories in this book. It is always a daunting experience to present one's writing to a large audience. Because of their generosity, I am able to explain and demonstrate the process of writing more clearly.

Thank you to the teachers of DeKalb County Central United Schools, in northeast Indiana, who have opened their classrooms to me and welcomed my suggestions. I especially appreciated Cheryl Weaver's hospitality and enthusiasm while I worked through the story-writing process with her students. I owe a special gratitude to Connie Fullerton, who offers weekly, and sometimes daily, support to this effort by discussing her observations of her student writers with me.

Thank you to the principal and staff at Harlan Elementary School, in Harlan, Indiana, for their contributions while exploring story writing. Thank you, as well, to Debbie Williams and her seventh-grade students at the Canterbury School, in Ft. Wayne, Indiana, for their willingness to test new waters and share the results.

Of course, this book was written and published under the direct guidance of caring editors, Wendy Murray and Joanna Davis-Swing. From the initial phone call through the six months of writing and revision, they have both been gentle, steady mentors.

I am most thankful for my family members' constant support and encouragement. Without their patience, I would never have been able to produce a book of this scope. It is always the humanity of others that brings art to its fullest measure.

*Lola Schaefer is available for one to three-day staff development workshops on teaching story in grades 1–8.
You may contact her through Scholastic, at the address listed below.*

Front cover and interior design by Kathy Massaro
Cover photograph by Joan Beard
Interior photographs courtesy of the author

ISBN 0-439-11757-7
Copyright © 2001 by Lola M. Schaefer, all rights reserved.
Printed in the USA

CONTENTS

FOR THE PAST EIGHTEEN YEARS, I have been helping children write narratives, or stories. At first, I provided ideas, and they fulfilled these assignments. Some stories were delightful, but most lacked pizzazz. Later, my students wrote the stories *they wanted to write.* And guess what? The quality of the stories improved, but then, so did my instruction. I wasn't telling them what to write; rather, I was modeling and guiding them through writing strategies to create characters, settings, and plots.

Now I am working in schools as a writing consultant. It's a new challenge, but I've learned that the approach to teaching writing that I've developed holds up, whether I'm working with kindergartners or eighth graders. We examine well-written stories and identify their strengths. Together we work through the writing process, from purpose and audience to story plan and final draft. Along the way, we practice strategies for developing strong stories.

So how did I get from there to here? from using teacher-directed story prompts to helping children learn how to develop their own stories and narrative voices? The route was paved by the usual trial and error, professional development, and something serendipitous: my own creative writing.

When I began to explore my own writing goals—namely, writing picture books—I was amazed by the wealth of information available to aspiring authors of children's books. Immediately I could see how many of these tricks of the trade would be valuable for classroom teachers. As I attended writing conferences, I was further impressed by how these tips for creating stories could be easily grasped by children. And so this book is a blend of strategies handed down from the masters and my know-how as a teacher and writer. Peppered throughout these chapters are references to the books that have provided me with the most important ideas and insights.

I have written the book for teachers of intermediate grades, in the hope that you and your students will enjoy many of the rich experiences that foster a love of story writing. Refer to this book once, twice, as many times as you need, to cement your own practice of story writing. Keep it in the classroom. Let it support you and your students so that together you achieve growth and satisfaction with each new story.

Setting Expectations for Growth

s teachers, we know the power stories have on children (and ourselves, too). It is apparent every time we read aloud a story to the class, and notice the enraptured expressions on our students' faces. As adults, we know that story is the fabric that holds us together, and we know this more deeply than our students ever could. Everything we hear

These 4th grade students and I are working on strong leads during a mini-lesson.

and read, from telephone chatter to e-mail to international news to dinner conversations to family traditions, is nothing more than story. It is what our lives are all about. A well-written story carries us deep into the human experience and connects us with others in a way that defies explanation. As Marion Dane Bauer, author of *What's Your Story?*, says at the outset of her book, "Stories help us to make sense of our world. They teach us what is possible. They let us know that others before us have struggled as we do."

As readers, whether we tend to enjoy novels or nonfiction, we appreciate the way skilled writers string words together to fill us with emotion and wonder. *What a gift! How do they do that?* we might ask ourselves after reading a powerful passage. The truth is, accomplished writers work at their craft. They are collectors of words, musicians of rhythm, engineers of plot, and, most importantly, human beings who want to share a good story. This is what we need to understand, and what we need to help our students understand. Writers work at their craft.

Whenever I read an interview with an author, they often remark that self-expression is their one true purpose for writing. This is something to keep in mind as we teach our children to write stories. But while self-expression must be at the forefront of any writing endeavor in the classroom, we need to explicitly teach students the critical skills necessary to express themselves well. We need to guide students to

- know they have stories worth telling and that their understandings of the world are important to themselves and others.
- understand the structure of stories.
- use the conventions of language to communicate meaning.
- practice the steps in organizing, writing, and revising a story.
- learn and use strategies that will help them to write focused stories with strong characters, authentic problems, and believable resolutions.
- read stories as writers (critically and thoughtfully).

This need for modeling and guided practice is something I learned the hard way. The first few years I taught, I assumed that reading a batch of good stories was all the preparation students needed to be successful writers. What was I thinking? I knew from my own life experiences that practice and more practice were essential when learning anything new. Now I model every step of the writing process, and in fact share the phases of the writing process with children at the outset of our writing journey.

Describing the Writing Process

One of the first things I want children to understand is that the writing process is recursive in design. This means that a writer doesn't move through each step once, never to return. Instead, a writer uses a certain process to progress through and revisit essential stages to ultimately produce a strong piece of writing.

Of all the graphic organizers I've used to illustrate the writing process for students, I like a circle best, because it reminds me of the cycles in nature. After an animal, plant, river, or planet goes through a cycle, it—or an offspring—returns, ready to begin anew. I like to think that if we support children through the writing process correctly, they will return renewed, ready to begin again.

The Writing Process

Select Topic

Determine Audience, Choose Form of Writing

Share with an Audience

Create a Plan

Publish

Communicate Meaning

Write a Rough Draft

Edit and Proofread

Revise for Meaning

Revise

Peer-Critique

I display this cycle big, in a conspicuous place where students can refer to it with ease. I also have a copy of it on an overhead transparency. I show it frequently to help children identify where they are in the process. I especially like to point out the many times we back up and revisit a stage while planning or writing.

When wall space is limited, I use the three-columns format shown below, but continually remind students that good writers revisit stages while writing.

Writing Process

Forming Intentions	Composing	Publishing
List Ideas	Write Rough Draft	Edit
Develop Ideas	Revise	Select Illustrative Style
Identify Purpose and Audience	Peer-Critique	Type or Write Final Story
Create a plan	Revise Again	Bind or Display
		Share With Audience and Observe Responses

A bold, visual reference to the writing process acts as a critical support for the students. It's a constant reminder that writing is a thoughtful, recursive engagement.

Shared readings of favorite books and discussions of authors' reflections on writing are other constant companions on our journey through the writing process. In particular, the works of Katherine Paterson, James Cross Giblin, Marion Dane Bauer, and Ralph Fletcher have sparked animated discussions (see box at left). Sometimes my students and I have merely agreed with what we've read and felt validated that we are on the same path as veteran writers. Other times, we've gained insights that have helped us question what we are doing, and we've made plans to experiment with new approaches.

It will take lots of time to carefully guide your students through the writing process. Each step will take much modeling and practice, but don't sacrifice this foundation-building work to move into independent writing too quickly! Every minute you invest at the beginning of the year will pay off later with stronger student writing. That is one important thing the children have taught me. Go slowly, understand what you're doing, and enjoy the journey!

Communicating Expectations for Growth

The teacher's attitude toward writing sets the classroom tone for growth and success. We need to know for ourselves the specific expectations we have for our students before they begin writing. We need to have a sense of how much writing counts in our classroom, and I don't mean in terms of the grades we give, but in terms of the energy and "heart" we plan to devote to writing. For example, I know that story cannot be taught in one class period; it needs to be part of an ongoing process that continues throughout the year. I know that students need to assume responsibility for their use of writing strategies. I also know that when students and I plan, write, critique, revise, and evaluate together, great growth can be documented.

Most important, we need to communicate to students the expectation that *everyone* will improve in the craft of writing story. I convey this in everything I say. For example:

Writing a story is hard work but I'm going to share some strategies that will help you enjoy the journey.

You will put a lot of problem-solving and time into your plans, but your stories will reflect this hard work.

I was so impressed with your last stories. Some of you had strong characters, and others had well-developed plots. It will be exciting to see how you grow as story writers in this next work.

Remember, our goal is to write our strongest story yet. Look back at your last story. Are there any weaknesses? What can you do differently in your plan and writing to strengthen your next story?

Model the Writing Process

Model every step of the writing process so your students can observe you. Watching you in action—whether writing at the overhead projector or during another writerly moment—stirs good student questions: They may wonder, *How does this writer think? What is this writer doing? Can I try that in my next story?* Comprehension begins only if the students are actively engaged. Have them help you narrow your topic, enlist their aid in creating a story plan—or critique your plan before you begin writing. Ask them to identify your strongest vocabulary, signs of character growth, and episodes of

Ben and Caity compare their final rubric assessment of Ben's short story.

plot development—but beware! You must set your ego aside: Students will be kind but candid with their suggestions!

Three of the teachers I coached this past year had never modeled planning and writing for their students. After many weeks of working in front of the children with overhead projectors, they shared their students' suggestions with me:

⚙ *"While I'm working on a plan, the students want me to add more conflict to my episodes."*

⚙ *"My students are frustrated because they think my endings are too predictable. They continually offer me alternative ideas to add cleverness to my writing."*

⚙ *"At first my students thought my writing was boring. They have encouraged me to take risks—to try a stronger voice. And I have. In the past, I thought there was only one way to write—like a textbook. Now my writing actually sings at times."*

Take Time to Be Thoughtful

One insight I have gained from working with the students is that more time should be spent thinking through the different stages together. When modeling and class collaboration are expanded, teachers and students experiment side by side, learning how to problem-solve through the sticky areas of a plan. Story writing is a thoughtful process. Let's provide a protective environment in which students can practice thinking and at the same time grow as story writers.

The Role of Mini-Lessons

Mini-lessons are brief, highly focused meetings in which the teacher, a professional writer, or a student models for the other learners the use of a writing strategy. Ideally, mini-lessons bubble up in class on an as-needed basis. In other words, as you work at your writing, you will notice opportunities to come together and study specific aspects of the craft. This doesn't mean that a mini-lesson is always successful in solving a writer's dilemma, but at the very least it provides a ringside seat, so to speak, from which students can watch another writer address a problem.

There is no set schedule for mini-lessons, but I find that including at least two a week is ideal. I favor introducing them at the beginning of writing time; a mini-lesson is a strong transition between the business of the classroom and the quiet reflective time children need for writing. I ask that all students relax and give full attention to the presenter. Many children make notes in their notebooks to refer to later about the strategy.

As teachers, we need to be constantly on the lookout for mini-lesson topics. Observe students' progress and difficulties. Watch them as they work, listen to them confer, and note their needs when you read their pieces. Look for that prime time to teach a matter of craft. For instance, present a mini-lesson on "strong beginnings" when students have drafted their story openings. You may say, "Remember that a strong beginning engages the reader from the first sentence. The story doesn't begin until there is action." You might place one or two examples of strong beginnings from published works on the overhead. To highlight their strengths, you might also include one beginning that is a little weaker and in need of revision. Let students come up to the overhead and circle those sentences or phrases that immediately grab their attention and have them explain why. Discuss these observations and what can be done to strengthen the weaker story beginning so that it draws the reader in more quickly. To end the mini-lesson, you may give them this charge: "Please reread your beginnings today. Ask yourself, *Will the reader be involved and care after my first three sentences?* If not, you may want to rework your openings."

Invite Professional Writers to Give Mini-Lessons

I have had published writers come to the classroom and give 15- to 20-minute mini-lessons on some of the "tricks" of a particular genre.

For instance, if the class is writing historical fiction, an author might discuss how to weave factual information into the setting so that it lends authenticity without overwhelming the story. A writer of successful picture books could lead a mini-lesson on how a few carefully chosen words can evoke as much emotion as an entire paragraph. A mystery writer might share tips on how to build suspense. Sometimes just having a new writer's face in the classroom adds a dash of excitement to the process.

Student-Led Mini-Lessons

Students themselves can lead successful mini-lessons. During small critique sessions, children readily recognize the strengths of their fellow writers. Informally they consult these peers one-on-one to ask advice. Invite students to share their insights with the class. If they have a specific strategy they've had success with, ask them to elaborate on it or, if they prefer, to prepare a mini-lesson for the next time you meet.

One of my fifth-grade students demonstrated a unique illustration technique to the class. Another child demonstrated how she planned her cumulative story. One boy shared aloud with the class his method of increasing tension in his stories.

Mini-lessons That Inspire

Sometimes a mini-lesson is needed during the writing period simply to invigorate the writing community. In her book *The Art of Teaching Writing* (Heinemann, 1994), Lucy Calkins summarizes the value of mini-lessons:

> *We need to think of mini-lessons, then, as ways of adding information to the class pot. If five children use an idea when it is presented and others merely jot it in a list of possible strategies at the back of their writer's notebook, that idea is nevertheless in the room. When those five children share their work, the idea will be recirculated. Meanwhile, other children have tucked the idea into the back of their minds, and they may draw upon it when they need it.*

Rubrics

Like mini-lessons, rubrics are a tool I use regularly in my teaching. I love to use them, and so do the students. Rubrics set writing standards for a particular piece, guide students during the process, and later work as a means of self-assessment. There are a variety of styles, but the form I rely upon is an easy grid. Here is one basic example:

Name _____ Date _____

Story Title _____

Story Rubric

	EXCELLENT	GOOD	NEEDS WORK
Complete Plan	a brief plan with all story elements	a brief plan with some story elements	incomplete plan
Character	believable and likable	one or the other	neither believable nor likable
Setting	where and when	one or the other	neither where nor when
Problem	a problem the character can solve believable	one or the other	neither
Beginning, Middle, and End	All three can be found in the story.	Two of the three can be found in the story.	One of the three can be found in the story.

131

How Students Use Rubrics

The term *rubric* can sound daunting, but really, a rubric is user-friendly. Here's a snapshot of how one is often used in my classroom: A rubric at his side, a student rereads his or her completed story and evaluates it based on a rubric's list of 3 to 5 criteria. Next, a peer reads that same writing *twice* and evaluates the piece again. If there are differences, the two students substantiate their assessments with direct references to the text until both agree on the same evaluation.

Never doubt the power of this peer review! One group of seventh graders told me they learned even more about short-story writing through this evaluation procedure than they did from any lessons. Why? They felt that when they had to support their assessment with direct references, it made them think more analytically about what they had written and how they would write in the future. They also mentioned how much easier it is to be objective and critical of someone else's writing than their own. These "ah-ha!"'s are what truly cement learning.

Name _____ Date _____

Story Title _____

Personal Story

	EXCELLENT	GOOD	NEEDS WORK
Focus on One Incident	The writing consistently focuses on one incident from beginning to end.	Most of the writing focuses on one incident.	The writing never fully describes one incident.
Vocabulary	six or more strong, specific words	four or five strong, specific words	three or fewer strong, specific words
Character, Setting, Problem, Resolution	It is easy to identify the characters, setting, problem, and resolution.	The story contains a main character, setting, and problem.	The story contains only one or two story elements.
Varied Sentence Structure	Three or more different sentence structures are used throughout the story.	Two different sentence structures are used.	The same sentence structure is used throughout the story.

Teaching Narrative Writing: The Tools That Work for Every Student Scholastic Professional Books

Collaborating to Create a Rubric

During the first few years I used rubrics, my students and I would all sit down together after each having finished a story. I would ask them what kinds of things they had tried to accomplish within those stories. Usually they listed five to seven items. From those we narrowed the choices to three to five of the most significant. We wrote each of these down the left-hand column of a rubric. Together we created standards for each item and wrote these under "Excellent," "Good," and "Needs Work." The students were then able to evaluate their stories against the rubrics.

	EXCELLENT	GOOD	NEEDS WORK

Create a Rubric Before the Pen Hits the Paper

One day a fifth-grade student suggested, "If we could create the rubrics *before* we begin planning our story, we would do a better job of working toward those standards." Yes, from the mouths of babes. So now, unless my time is limited by a classroom demonstration, the students and I develop the rubrics before they begin their writing. I stand at the overhead with a transparency of an open rubric, and they each have a copy at their seat. It looks like the one at left.

More Tips for Defining Criteria

At the beginning of the year, I use only three levels of proficiency across the top so the students can ease into the use of rubrics. After they have become familiar with the procedure, I add a fourth proficiency. The headings usually read: "Excellent," "Good," "OK," and "Needs Work." It is interesting to note that I have never had a student fall into the "Needs Work" category when the rubric has been created before the writing.

In my opinion, it is counterproductive to have more than five areas of growth marked on one rubric. I use the word *growth* intentionally, because that is the main purpose of rubrics—to show students their growth as writers. The term *rubric* has never carried a negative meaning with my students. Instead, they see it as support to help identify their strengths and weaknesses.

Rubrics need to favor the elements of craft, rather than the mechanics of language. For story, the criteria can be:

- focus
- meaning
- vocabulary
- beginning, middle, end
- character development
- plot development
- believable and solid resolution
- thoughtful title
- show, not tell

- illustrations that add meaning (published story)
- clarity/fluency
- voice
- use of descriptive language (metaphor, simile)
- historical setting
- elements of a tale
- elements of fantasy

There is a slight hierarchy in the importance of these elements. *Focus* and *meaning* are essential to all writing, so you will want to include these elements on a rubric at the beginning of the year. *Word choice, story form,* and *story elements* are also fundamental to story construction, so these ought to appear on the rubric as well. Add some of the finer points of story construction, like *voice* and *descriptive language* to the rubric when you've introduced them to students. What students choose to put on the rubric will depend upon the genre, too; for example, when developing a rubric for a cumulative story, the criteria might include *tight focus* and *language carries a rhythm*.

All rubrics need to place some importance on the mechanics. If a student writes a strong story, poor punctuation or spelling could detract from the meaning. These are the criteria most commonly used in our rubrics:

- spelling
- grammar
- punctuation

- varied sentence structure
- correct paragraphing

Remind students frequently that we revise to clarify meaning and edit to correct mechanics. If the writer does not create a jewel of a story there is no reason to polish it for public view. Most of the writing process is geared toward writing a strong story that is focused, carries meaning, and entertains. Only when the writer has accomplished that will he edit for publication.

Since we want to keep rubrics user-friendly, I suggest never using a grid larger than 4 x 5. If the rubric becomes complicated, students get sidetracked with worry about meeting the numerous criteria. Instead, I recommend keeping the rubrics simple, especially at the beginning of the year. A 3 x 4 grid allows students to focus on four characteristics to use as personal writing goals, as a point of reference during critique and revision, and later as criteria by which they assess their piece. When you see students are comfortable using this rubric, move them on to a 4 x 4 grid. Students in grades seven and eight can quickly move to a 4 x 5 grid as their expertise grows.

With each piece of writing and each genre of writing, the criteria can be modified. (See pages 131–132 for more rubrics.) Students score their writing proficiency by placing an X over the box that describes their level of performance. If a grade needs to be assigned to an occasional story, a number system can be used to evaluate the different proficiencies, and a percentage grade can be computed. I prefer to use the rubrics themselves as final assessments of success.

A Rubric's Role in Portfolio Selection and Reflection

Many classrooms manage both writing folders and portfolios separately. For me, simplicity is best. My students were encouraged to use large spiral notebooks that served as their writing workbooks for the semester, or year. They wrote and drew all brainstorming diagrams, ideas, prewriting, research, plans, and rough drafts in these. The classroom rule for us was: *Don't ever tear it out because it might get lost.*

Each month, the students chose a piece of writing to add to their portfolios, which contained student-selected work from all curriculum subjects. They could add more, if they wanted, throughout the month, but one selection was mandatory. After pieces were chosen, they included the plan, the rough draft, the final draft, and the rubric. That way, there was a visual record of how the writing developed. All pieces were dated and stapled together with the rubric on top.

During the last five years of my teaching, I had parent/teacher conferences with each student. In fact, the students managed the conferences themselves with my guidance. During one part, a student would independently select five different pieces from his portfolio that he wanted to discuss with his parents. Inevitably, these selections included at least one set of rubrics, if not more. Intrigued, I would later ask my students why they favored rubrics. Their answers were so sincere:

* "Rubrics show quickly what I do well as a writer and what I need to work on."

* "I like rubrics because I and another student decide on the evaluation."

* "My parents don't know what rubrics are. I like to show them I know more about my learning than they do."

* "I can show them exactly what I was doing in September and later in November as a writer."

* "Rubrics were very useful to me for writing future stories. They taught me what I needed to work on—what my strengths and weaknesses were. I wanted to show my parents where I was in the process."

Using Rubrics to Inform Your Teaching

It is important for teachers to review the writing students select for their portfolios and to understand the students' own criteria for selection. It offers insight into what they've put into practice and what further mini-lessons they may need. If I notice that many students are developing strong characters that resolve their own problems, I know we will not need to do much more work in that area; but if I see quick story resolutions without much episodic development, I can design a series of mini-lessons to offer practice in building tension. We can analyze short passages from published books to study how professional writers create conflict. We can work and rework a series of events as a class until we are pleased that the story is building in tension. The students themselves are the best source for your next mini-lesson.

Noticing What Students Value

Sometimes I felt discouraged when I saw what my students were including in their portfolios. Their choices weren't always what I felt was their strongest work. When I asked them, however, they could articulate the reasons for their selections. For the most part, my students valued cleverness. Even if the selected stories, poems, or narratives weren't exceptionally strong, students could immediately point out the clever elements that made them special in their eyes. Sometimes it was an enticing lead that set the emotional stage for a story. In other instances, it was a well-crafted ending that pulled it together in an unusual way. In these cases, the students surprised themselves with their own writing. I know that feeling as a writer—it's powerful! These leaps of inspired writing are never anticipated; they just come out of the blue and need to be celebrated. I always smile when a student says, "This is like something a real author would write." Some of my students chose the pieces whose rubrics reflected their highest levels of proficiency; but for most, the decision was more personal. Sometimes subject matter was the reason one piece appealed to them over another. Other times, the decision was based on how easily a story came together and, ultimately, how pleasurable the process of writing it was.

Including a Reflection Piece on the Rubric

It became apparent to me that I wanted the children to reflect on their choices. So I asked them to write one or two sentences on the bottom of the rubric, explaining their selections. I asked them to be as specific as possible. This small reflection enabled students to see what they valued. They, too, noticed that they didn't always select the piece with the strongest rubric rating but rather one that held personal appeal. Eventually, after continued practice, you and the students will see selections that reflect both quality construction and personal appeal. It takes time and patience and an expectation for growth.

H ere are comments that Lindie Hohler, the fifth-grade author of *A Time of Hope*, (see excerpt in Chapter 10) wrote about her piece of historical fiction:

"In my story, I'm proud of my interesting plot. After two weeks of research, I decided to focus on Cleopatra's final moments. I explored realistic ways that Cleopatra came to receive an asp for the purpose of committing suicide. Also, I think I really captured what it would have been like if my character, Marcus Conpolion, had existed. My favorite part of the story is when Marcus and Jericho are trying to catch the asp. I really wrote what a 12-year-old boy would have been doing in that situation."

The Lifeblood of Writing

W hen students and I discussed their portfolio selections, we agreed that writers naturally choose the pieces that offer them the greatest personal satisfaction. This reminded me once again that for all my efforts with language use, punctuation, sentence structure, and paragraphing, it is *meaning* and *self-expression* that fuel a writer's heart. That doesn't mean it's a waste of time to teach the mechanics, but it is another reminder that helping students craft strong, personal stories takes precedence; later on, they will care much more about polishing them for an audience.

Students also informally began asking one another if certain pieces had been chosen for their portfolios. This is another outgrowth of the writing community. Every student becomes familiar with the writing of others. They invest time and effort through readings, critiques, revisions, and edits. When they become attached to a piece of writing, they hope the writer himself likes it, too.

Now that we have explored the underpinnings of the writing community and the classroom routines and tools that set expectations for growth, let's step into practice. Literature and writing are two inseparable threads of the story fabric. We need to deftly weave the two together and offer our students the best understanding of both.

CHAPTER 2

Understanding Story Elements

Seventh grader Caity Kelly listens to a mini-lesson on writing story summaries.

To build a firm footing for future writing, students need to identify story elements in literature. Throughout the year, read picture books and study how these stories are put together, using a story summary framework as a guide. (Later on, if you feel your students are ready, use novels with more involved but not overly intricate plot structures.)

A story summary is a great tool for helping students recognize the main events in a story and their sequence. Each summary begins with a one-sentence encapsulation of the beginning of the book, the main character, the setting, and a hint of the problem. Another sentence describes the ending and shows the resolution of the problem. For the middle of the story, three episodes are selected that involve the struggle or conflict of the story.

The first few times students write summaries, they will benefit from making a brief plan first. This gives them the opportunity to identify the events that represent the beginning, middle, and end of a story. The plan becomes a handy organizational map to refer to when writing the summary.

Model Lesson: Summarizing *Cinderella*

To introduce story summaries, use a story that all your students know. Begin by modeling at the overhead the writing of a plan for a five-sentence summary. Slowly, thinking out loud, walk the students through the steps.

For the story *Cinderella*, the modeling of writing a plan might go as follows:

Teacher: What happened at the beginning of the story? Who did what?

[teacher writes]:

Cinderella's stepsisters and stepmother—cruel. (beginning)

Teacher: How did this story end? Who did what?

[teacher writes]:

Prince searched—wed Cinderella. (end)

[Now I list three major events that make up the middle of the story.]

Teacher: How did Cinderella meet and marry the prince?

[teacher writes]:

Royal ball announced. (conflict introduced—middle)

Teacher: Did Cinderella go to the ball?

[teacher writes]:

Stepmother and stepsisters went—Cinderella had chores. (conflict continues—middle)

Teacher: How did Cinderella meet the Prince?

[teacher writes]:

Fairy godmother—Cinderella danced with Prince. (conflict heightens—middle)

While modeling out loud, I deliberately ask questions about the minor details of the story.

Teacher: What chores did the evil stepmother and stepsisters give Cinderella?
What did the fairy godmother do to help Cinderella get to the royal ball?
How did the Prince find Cinderella?

Thinking aloud, I offer answers to these last three questions, but I don't write them down on the overhead transparency. I say, "These details might add pizzazz to the story, but they are not events essential to the story line. Since a summary is a retelling of the *main* story elements, I'm not going to include this extra information." Students need to watch us think and evaluate. My last step is to order the final five events according to how they happened in the story. My final plan would look like this:

- Cinderella's stepsisters and stepmother—cruel.
- Royal ball announced.
- Stepmother and stepsisters went—Cinderella had chores.
- Fairy godmother—Cinderella danced with Prince.
- Prince searched—wed Cinderella.

Notice that the plan is brief, simple, and uses short phrases instead of complete sentences. If it becomes too elaborate, students will want to skip this part of the story-writing process. As you'll see throughout this book, a plan is an essential tool for focused writing; we don't want kids to reject it because it's too laborious.

Modeling the Summary

Now, I'm ready to write my summary. Keeping my plan on the overhead projector, where the students can watch me refer to it, I begin writing a draft. Using rich vocabulary, I retell the important story events as fluently as I can. When I have completed my rough draft, I reread my summary out loud:

"Cinderella"

Cinderella lived in a beautiful house with her stepmother
and stepsisters, who didn't like her and were mean to her.
It was announced that the palace was hosting a royal ball for the Prince,
so the stepsisters spent days in preparation.
Cinderella's stepmother kept her busy with difficult chores.
Cinderella's fairy godmother appeared and helped her get to the palace,
where Cinderella danced with the Prince.
He was so charmed by Cinderella that he used all
his resources to find her.

Model Revision

Since we want students to know that writers rarely get it down perfect on their first draft, I purposely reread and look for weak areas to revise. "Does the summary include all the information in my plan?" I ask my students. Then we go through each line of the plan, looking for corresponding information in the summary. Students find direct matches until the final sentence. In this case the summary does not mention that the Prince wed Cinderella, so with a different-colored marker, I add that information to my first draft: *He was so charmed by Cinderella that he used all his resources to find her in the following days, and to make her his wife.*

Improve on Details

Next I go back and reread the summary a second time, asking the students if I can improve on vocabulary or details. Someone might mention that the stepsisters didn't like Cinderella because she was pretty and they were not. Another might ask me to show how they were mean to her. Again I make a simple revision in color on my first draft: *Cinderella lived in a beautiful house with her stepmother and stepsisters, who resented her beauty and treated her as a servant.*

Polish, Rewrite, and Display

I might ask if there are any changes needed in the third line to add detail to that part of the story. A student might suggest writing that the stepmother refused to let Cinderella go to the ball. The revision could look like this: *Cinderella's stepmother would not allow her to go to the ball and kept her busy with difficult chores.*

I then reread the text with the revisions and ask students if it is now a thorough summary. After getting their approval, I rewrite or type that summary and place it—and the plan—on display in the classroom for reference:

"Cinderella"

Cinderella lived in a beautiful house with her stepmother and stepsisters, who resented her beauty and treated her as a servant.
It was announced that the palace was hosting a royal ball for the Prince, so the stepsisters spent days in preparation. Cinderella's stepmother would not allow her to go and kept her busy with difficult chores. Cinderella's fairy godmother appeared and helped her get to the palace, where Cinderella danced with the Prince. He was so charmed by Cinderella that he used all his resources to find her in the following days, and to make her his wife.

What the Demonstration Accomplished

Three positive effects come from this exercise. First, the teacher enters the writing community by working in front of the class and inviting comments. Second, the students observe a writer at work, using a plan to organize thoughts so that her final piece is meaningful, focused, and fluent. Third, the students learn the framework for planning, writing, and revising their own stories in the future. Modeling this process isn't enough. We need to actually *tell* students that these experiences will prepare them to write strong stories of their own.

Practice Writing Summaries Collaboratively

After this experience, students are ready to write five-sentence summaries collaboratively. This doesn't mean I never model this practice again; it depends on the group of children. After working through one summary together, you'll be able to assess their understanding of the process. Here is an example of a plan and summary developed collaboratively by a group of fifth graders after reading *The Log Cabin Quilt* by Ellen Howard:

Plan

⚙ Elvirey and family move to Michigan. (who, what, where—beginning)

⚙ Granny—quilt—Pap—cabin. (struggle starts—middle)

⚙ Elvirey and sister chink. (struggle continues—middle)

⚙ Storm pushes mud out. (struggle heightens—middle)

⚙ Elvirey chinks with cloth. (resolution—end)

Summary

Elvirey's Mam dies, and Pap takes the family from Carolina to Michigan by wagon. Granny pieces scraps into a quilt while Pap builds a cabin. Elvirey and her sister chink the log cabin's walls with mud and the family moves in. While Pap is gone hunting, a hard winter storm hits and pushes the frozen mud out of the logs. Elvirey uses Grandma's scraps to chink the logs from the inside, adding warmth, color, and memories of Mam to the cabin.

Mentoring in Action

Modeling is essential at all stages of teaching story development. This kind of "working out loud" at the overhead projector or chalkboard makes the writing process visible for students. After the demonstration, have the class participate in the process collaboratively. This whole-group practice helps students refine their understanding of the different steps. They may need to practice and talk through a strategy several times before they are ready to work independently.

Partner Practice

Have students write plans and summaries in the same manner you've modeled. You may wish to have them work with partners first, before working on their own. Each team can select a picture book, read it, and take turns summarizing the book orally. (Instruct one partner to repeat the summary to show he is listening carefully.) The partners can then write a summary together.

I find it's helpful to keep the guide questions posted on the overhead projector: *What happened at the beginning of the story? What happened at the*

Chase Sizemore, fourth grader
Shiloh by Phyllis Reynolds Naylor

▲▲▲▲▲▲▲▲▲ ▲ ▲▲▲▲▲▲▲▲▲

Plan

- Summer—West Virginia—Marty finds dog—Shiloh. (who, what, where beginning)
- Marty thinks Shiloh's master, Judd, kicks his dogs. (what—conflict begins—middle)
- Marty keeps Shiloh a secret. (conflict continues—middle)
- Marty works for Judd. (conflict continues—middle)
- Marty gets to keep Shiloh as his own. (resolution—end)

Summary

It was a summer day in West Virginia when Marty found a beagle that he named Shiloh. It followed him back home, and Marty started feeding Shiloh. Marty thought Judd, Shiloh's master, kicked his dogs. Marty kept Shiloh a secret from his mom, dad, and especially Judd, who wanted his dog back. Marty started working for Judd and ended up keeping Shiloh as his own.

Notice how focused Chase remained in his summary. He added a little information that was not in his plan, but was able to keep his five main points.

end of the story? What three important things happened in the middle of the story? Each team can look at the first question, talk through what needs to be said, and then write that action in one concise sentence at the top of their page. They repeat the process for the second question, this time writing the sentence at the bottom of the page. Their responses to the third question get written in the middle of the page. If students need to cut and tape the middle events in the correct sequence, allow time for that. Talking through and writing a summary together can take 15 to 30 minutes.

Student Plan and Summary

Erica Wilson, seventh grader
Running Out of Time by Margaret Peterson Haddix

Plan

- Jessie—12—1840 historic preserve—really 1996. (who, where—beginning)
- Disease sweeps through village. (what—struggle begins—middle)
- Jessie—medicine—real world. (struggle continues—middle)
- Jessie—unaware of modern inventions—bad people. (struggle continues—middle)
- Jessie—courage—bring help. (resolution—end)

Summary

Jessie, a twelve-year-old girl, lives in an 1840 historic preserve and has no idea that it is actually 1996 in the "real world." She is told by her mother that a horrible disease is sweeping through their village. She asks Jessie to escape and get modern medicine and help for all the sick children. But the real trouble is, Jessie has never seen a telephone, car, or anything invented after 1840. Jessie uses her courage to make her way through the sometimes confusing and evil world to save the village.

Paring Down the Summary to Three Sentences

The next step is to help students summarize a story in just three sentences. This step helps students learn to define a story's conflict. To model this, I place a transparency of the five-sentence summary for *Running Out of Time* on the overhead projector.

Teacher: Would you like to use the same first and last sentences for your new summary?

Class: Yes.

Teacher: Okay, then let's see if we can write the conflict in one sentence. Let's reread the three middle events that describe the conflict. Since we can't include all that detail in our middle sentence, we need to identify the most important information. Who are we writing about?

Class: Jessie.

Teacher: What is her problem or struggle?

Class: She needs to get medicine for the sick children.

Teacher: What is getting in her way?

Class: She isn't aware of how things work in 1996.

Teacher: Great. Can we combine those three pieces of information into one sentence?

[class collaborates and comes up with]:

Jessie is sent out of the village to get modern medicine
to save sick children, even though she is not aware of how things work.

Teacher: Let's put all of our sentences together and see if we might want to revise any of the summary:

Jessie, a twelve-year-old girl, lives in an 1840 historic preserve
and has no idea that it is actually 1996 in the real world.
Jessie is sent out of the village to get modern medicine to save sick
children, even though she is not aware of how things work.
Jessie uses her courage to make her way through the sometimes
confusing and evil world to save the village.

At this point in the lesson, I would then ask two different students to read the summary out loud to the group. Then I'd ask, "Does this summary tell us the beginning, middle, and end? Did your ear hear anything that needs to be changed to help the summary make the most sense or read more smoothly?" Students might point out that they don't like that the word *Jessie* leads every sentence. Together, we'd come up with alternatives, and I'd write them on the overhead.

Here are some more sample plans and summaries you can use with your students:

Amanda Bok, sixth grader
Painting the Wind by Michelle Dionetti

Plan

- Arles, France—dislike—Vincent van Gogh. (who, where, what—beginning)
- Claudine—thinks differently. (struggle—middle)
- Vincent—leaving—shares painting. (resolution—end)

Summary

Most everyone in the city of Arles, France, dislikes Vincent van Gogh and thinks he is dangerous. But Claudine, Vincent's young friend, thinks differently. As Vincent gets ready to leave Arles, he shares a painting of a sunflower with Claudine.

Lilly's Purple Plastic Purse
by Kevin Henkes

Plan

- Lilly—new things—school—interrupts learning.
  (who, what, where—beginning)
- Teacher confiscates—Lilly angry—nasty note and picture.
  (struggle—middle)
- Lilly apologizes—class celebrates things—sharing time.
  (resolution—end)

Summary

Lilly takes her new purse, sunglasses, and quarters to school and interrupts learning when she shows them to her friends. Mr. Slinger, the teacher, confiscates Lilly's new things, which makes her so angry, she sends him a nasty note and picture. The next day, Lilly apologizes for her poor actions, and Mr. Slinger joins the class in a fun celebration of Lilly's prized possessions during sharing time.

Encourage Paraphrasing

Do not let children copy sentences directly from the text. While modeling and working collaboratively, stress the importance of shutting the book and writing the summary in original language. Use the book only as a reference to remember the sequence or specific events.

Find the Focus: Writing One-Sentence Summaries

Finally, have your students write an entire story line in one clear, concise sentence. A one-sentence summary states the focus of the story succinctly. All the other actions and details help develop this story line. Later, when students want to develop a focus for their stories, this practice will help them be successful. To model this, put one of your three-sentence summaries on the overhead, and together, pare it down to a single sentence. For example, for the story *Running Out of Time*, a one-sentence summary might read:

Jessie, a twelve-year-old girl, leaves her home in an 1840s historic village and finds medicine in the real world to save children.

Even a one-sentence summary contains the specific *who, where, what*, and a bit of the resolution. An excellent resource for one-sentence summaries can be found on the Cataloging-in-Publication, or CIP page, at the beginning of any published book. Below is an example from *Preacher's Boy* by Katherine Paterson:

In 1899, ten-year-old Robbie, son of a preacher in a small Vermont town, gets himself into all kinds of trouble when he decides to give up being Christian in order to make the most of his life before the end of the world.

This exercise is especially important in the early stages of story writing, but should be revisited several times throughout the year. You will be impressed by your students' growth and the impact this exercise has on their abilities to organize and craft stories.

Display the Summaries

Sharing finished work is a vital part of the writing process. Students benefit not only from the input and praise of others but also from using their classmates' work as important references for their own future writing. Once your children have developed good summaries, have them review and select their most focused and clearly written pieces. Make these summaries available as class references by

- placing them in a display folder.
- making overhead transparencies of them.
- posting them in the classroom.
- rewriting them onto a large flip chart.

Share Summaries With Younger Grades

For additional practice, have your students write three- or five-sentence summaries of traditional tales for first or second graders. Print them in large bold letters and include bright, color illustrations. This gives your students an authentic purpose and a specific audience for their writing. Some of my students' favorites are: *The Three Billy Goats Gruff, The Three Little Pigs, Little Red Riding Hood,* and *Goldilocks and The Three Bears.*

The Power of Main Dramatic Questions

To further help students understand that the best stories they read—and write—have a single, dramatic focus, introduce main dramatic question (MDQ). I first learned of this planning technique at a children's writers' workshop in Chautauqua, New York, when two children's novelists explained how they used MDQs, and I've been using them ever since.

A MDQ is a brief question that a writer articulates for the story she plans. It pinpoints the story's main concern, and helps writers keep their eyes trained on the main character's quest. *At the end of the story, the question can be answered by the reader with a yes or no.*

For instance, the MDQ for *The Three Little Pigs* could be "Will the big bad wolf eat the three little pigs?" or "Will the three little pigs outsmart the wolf?" For the book *Crash* by Jerry Spinelli, it might be "Will Crash mature in his relationship with Penn Webb?" In Ann Rinaldi's *An Acquaintance With Darkness* the question "Will Emily Pigbush be able to live with someone she trusts now that her mother has died and left her alone?" describes the central dramatic point.

Model First

To ensure student success, begin by modeling a possible MDQ for a story you all know well. Then write other MDQ's collaboratively. Put your examples on chart paper and post them in the classroom as future resources. As with summaries, you will want to repeat this exercise throughout the year. Students tend to use the devices that are practiced the most frequently. Each time you revisit MDQ's, children will surprise you with their growth as readers and writers. Throughout the year, help students identify the MDQ in the books they read so that they can then create their own MDQ's when planning their stories.

Brief, one-on-one conferences with students are good opportunities for helping students pose MDQ's for their stories. For example, Marie, a fifth-grade student, created a plan for a story set in ancient Egypt during the reign of Tutankhamen. Her main character, Zahir, was a young boy who cared for the king's doves. One day, in anger, he let them escape. Marie wanted to make sure she remained focused during her writing. I helped her develop a main dramatic question:

Teacher: What will Zahir's problem be in your story?

Marie: He needs to find the doves and bring them back to the palace.

Teacher: When will King Tutankhamen realize the doves are gone?

Marie: When the afternoon bells ring and the King comes to listen to the doves coo.

Teacher: To write a MDQ, you need to write a question with the character's name and the problem. Do you have that information now?

Marie: Yes.

Marie then wrote this MDQ for her story:

Will Zahir find and return the king's doves before the dreaded bells ring?

Other MDQ's students have posed are:

- ❂ Will Penelope escape the wizard and rescue her brother?
- ❂ Can Kyle outsmart the school bully and gain respect?
- ❂ Will Benjamin, a Patriot, be able to remain loyal to his Tory family?

Make MDQ's Visible References

Students need to post their MDQ's in a highly visible place so that it is a constant reminder to them of the story's focus. Some students tape it on their writing workbooks or folders, others copy it in large print and tape it to their desks or writing tables. If the writer begins to add extraneous material to his piece, the teacher or peer coach can quickly refer him to his MDQ as an aid in determining how essential this new information is.

An MDQ is just one tool a writer might find helpful. After teaching story writing for many years, I have found that the more organizational devices students use, the greater their chances of writing strong, focused stories.

Share Your Own Writing

While teaching writing, it is essential that we maintain an active role through modeling. I know, it takes courage to stand in front of students and participate in every step of the process, but it is through our own experimentation that we learn the frustrations and satisfactions of writing. We begin to understand how critical a good plan is to successful writing. We learn that not everyone can sit and write on command—that some days need to be spent thinking, working on a character, or just reading to see how other writers work toward solutions.

I encourage every reader of this book to be brave and to take those first few steps. Begin with summaries and main dramatic questions. Write in front of the students, and post your work alongside theirs. You'll be surprised by their reactions. They are watching, listening, and learning with you. Together, you are now becoming a community of writers.

Generating Ideas and Story Charts

Fifth grader Tricia Conley adds her story idea to the Idea Board.

Where do writers find ideas? They find them in all sorts of places. In their memories, their hearts, during conversations, while daydreaming—and in the works of other writers. It is natural for writers to be influenced and inspired by other authors. Before students and I plan and write our stories, we discuss how a good story makes us feel and what kinds of books are passed on from one reader to another. Why? I want students to recognize the emotional impact that all good writing has on a reader. As a result of these discussions and their own engagement in the writing process, my students begin to "read like writers." They not only notice the idea behind the writing, but how the idea was developed. They become more critical readers, evaluating whether the author succeeded in entertaining his audience.

Make a place in the classroom where both you and your students can share recommended good books—a student-supervised bulletin board, for example. Or hang chart paper in the reading center, where students can write their favorite titles and why they think they enjoyed these books so much.

I also try to share insights on how published writers get ideas, develop plans, research, write, and revise. I make sure the students know that writing is work—that it takes discipline and almost never comes out perfect the first time. They love to learn that E. B. White rewrote the beginning of *Charlotte's Web* many, many times before he was pleased. They are interested in the advice of Avi: "I think you become a writer when you stop writing for yourself or your teacher and start thinking about readers." After they read Jean Fritz's biographies, they are amazed to find out she is more than eighty years old and still writing books that children enjoy.

Tips for Talking with Authors

Help students collect information on children's writers from published books and professional journals. Check out the different children's publishers' Web pages which often offer biographical sketches on their authors and illustrators. Knowing more about famous writers, their struggles and successes, is a great inspiration for writing.

A few of my favorite books are:

- *Meet the Authors and Illustrators: 60 Creators of Favorite Children's Books Talk About Their Work*, Volumes I and II by Deborah Kovacs
- *Lives of the Writers: Comedies, Tragedies* by Kathleen Krull
- *Author Talk: Conversations with Judy Blume…Et Al* by Leonard Marcus
- *The Art and Craft of Writing for Children* by William Zinsser

In addition, Scholastic produces an excellent Web page entitled Scholastic Author Studies:

http://teacher.scholastic.com/authorsandbooks/authors/index.htm

Students can read short bios on many of their favorite picture book and middle grade novel authors. They can also participate in live chats with authors.

Finding—and Sharing—Story Ideas

Coming up with a good idea for a story is often the toughest part of writing. For students, this can be a particularly frustrating endeavor. Who hasn't heard, "What can I write about?"? Why not beat the students to the punch and make sure they always have plenty of ideas in the waiting?

In the past, I taught students the technique of keeping a list of ideas in their writing folders. I've learned, though, that children who get ideas easily list them; those who struggle with reading and writing generally have blank pages unless the teacher assists them in brainstorming. To avoid this problem, I have a classroom collection of ideas on display at all times. I call this collection an "idea board," or our own "writer's notebook." These are *not* "pre-made" story starters, but ideas that emerge from class readings, discussions, and planning sessions.

One- to two-word entries, like "car accident," or "pioneer girl" are not story ideas—these are topics. You'll need to show students how to stretch these topics into ideas that include a *who, where,* and *what*. For instance, if a student offered "a shy football player" as a story idea, I might say:

Teacher: You already have the who—the shy football player. Where is the football player that his shyness becomes a problem? Try to think of a place that being shy would really get in the way.

Student: At an awards ceremony, or an after-game party, or on the school stage.

Teacher: Which one do you think could be the biggest problem for the football player?

Student: On the school stage.

Teacher: Why? What problem could make this football player the most nervous or anxious?

Student: He needs to make a speech to the whole school.

Teacher: Okay, so let's write this idea out, and you will have a good story idea to develop.

[writes]:

A shy football player learns he has to make a speech on the stage to the student body.

Generate Story Ideas
In Other Curriculum Areas

Other content areas of the curriculum can be great sources of inspiration for story ideas too. In my classroom, social studies explorations of the Westward Movement, American Revolution, and the Civil War tended to create a surge of story ideas. A study of natural phenomena in science class often enticed students to write great myths or tall tales. Math stories arose when students were learning ratios, fractions, decimals, and percentages. The idea board can house ideas from all over the curriculum.

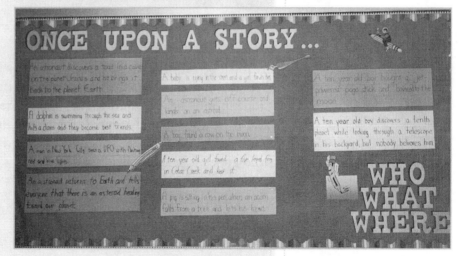

Above: Chris shows his friend, Tricia, the idea he wants to develop in his next story.

Right: This fifth grade idea board was generated after a study of the solar system. Story ideas range from science fiction to Just So stories to realistic fiction.

Exploring Life's Stories

Students rarely realize the wealth of stories in their own lives and that these stories even come equipped with beginnings, middles, and ends! That's exciting for them to discover, and our role is to help identify and develop them. It's a great place to start each year.

One way to access these stories is to invite moms, dads, grandparents, aunts, and uncles into your classroom for storytelling. Send home a letter that suggests possible themes, desired length of the storytelling, and the purpose of the activity. Purpose is very important—you want these families to know how you plan to use their experiences within the classroom. (See the Resource Pages sample letter.) For instance, you might tell them that you hope their visits will generate story ideas to add to the class idea board.

Borrowing Stories

If you're wondering if you should allow a student to write the exact life-story he hears, the answer is: yes! The inherent organization of these stories provides great support for students at this stage. A well-written story is always a delight, no matter where inspiration is found. Besides, many published authors record friends' or relatives' personal stories and include them in their books.

You'll be surprised to find out how many relatives will want to come into the classroom and share. An adaptation of this activity can be to have students interview a family member at home. They can then draw up a plan and write a short, well-focused story based on that interview. Here is a sixth-grade student's story, developed from an interview with her grandmother, who grew up in rural Nebraska.

Erica Wilson, sixth grader

Plan for "Playin' 'Possum":

Character: Lucille Tiller, age 11

Strengths: courageous, sly/quick-thinking

Flaw: gets angry easily when brothers push her around

Setting: Stockville, Nebraska, in Frontier County, 1943

Problem: Lucille's brothers, George and Bob, make her ride on the back of the horse when they are traveling to their grandmother's house, and she doesn't like it.

Episodes:
- Lucille rides on back of horse—feels taken advantage of.
- Falls off, plays 'possum—brothers scared she's dead.
- Gets to grandparents' house riding in the middle—brothers still nervous—Lucille proud.

Resolution: Lucille has satisfaction of convincing her brothers it's safer if she rides in the middle.

Growth: Even though she's younger, Lucille makes her brothers stop and think about what they're doing.

Erica Wilson, a sixth grader, works on her story plan for "Playin' 'Possum."

"Playin' 'Possum"

by Erica Wilson

It was one of those scorching Nebraska summer days—the kind of day when Mama likes us to visit Grandma and Grandpa Bush in Freedom. I don't mind much. In fact, in a way, I like to go there. Grandma always bakes us cookies and stirs up something cold to drink, and Grandpa likes to sit there and talk with us about the farm. When I got inside, out of the heat's fiery blaze, Papa was talking to Mama about the newspaper headlines.

"The heat wave of 1943 is comin', Myrtle, I knew it all along." I saw the paper, it said: "Frontier County Gazette reports a high reaching the 107-degree mark by Thursday."

"Why, right here in Stockville it's gotten up to 107 already. I guess you're right, Bill," Mama replied. After the interesting parts of their conversation were over, I ventured into the living room, where I saw Bob and George, my older brothers, wrestling. They love to do that. But they usually get yelled at by Mama. Sure enough, she came right at that very second and scolded them, but she also told me to go get Old Peg ready to go. She said we were going to Grandma and Grandpa's house. Papa suggested we go before it got too hot.

So I did as I was told and got Old Peg ready and out of her stall. I tied her up to our fence so I could go back inside and hurry up Bob and George. When we all three came bounding out of our house, Bob got Old Peg untied and hopped on her in the front, then I hurried to get up and sit in the middle. But George beat me to it. "Oohh," I growled under my teeth, "I have to sit in the back again? No, I'm, not..."

I was cut off by Bob. "Get on the back, or don't ride at all," he grumbled.

"Fine," I muttered and pulled myself up. It had been about twenty minutes, and I was getting squished. I felt like I was tricked, and I wouldn't put up with it anymore. So when we got to Bob's favorite ditch to trot over, I let go of George's waist and fell off—on purpose. It wasn't until they were over the ditch and a couple yards down that George realized I wasn't there. He asked, "Lucille, why aren't you holding on?" and when no one answered, he looked back and saw me lying lifeless in the

ditch. He shouted, "Bob, she fell off! Sis fell off!" He pointed
to me, and they both jumped off the horse. George raced over and
knelt beside me while Bob was tying Old Peg to a fence.

"Lucille. Wake up. C'mon, wake up," he said as he shook me.

Then Bob leapt over and whispered, "Is she dead? I didn't want
her to die. I really did like her." Then Bob leaned over and put
his ear to my mouth.

"Is she breathing?" George asked.

"Yes, as a matter of fact, she is. She tricked us, George, and
it's not funny, either."

"Oh, yes, it is," I replied as I slowly opened my eyes and
burst out laughing.

"Lucille, you scared us half to death," Bob said as he untied
Old Peg from the rusty fence.

"Yeah, but I taught you a lesson," I snapped back.

"Come on, let's go. At this pace, we'll never get to Granddad's
house," George scolded. So after Bob climbed up in the front on
Old Peg, I stepped up second, and George followed. When we got
to Grandma and Gramp's house, I must have had bruises all up the
sides of my waist, because George held on to me so tight, I knew
the only way I could ever fall off was with him with me.

"Oh, sweetie pies, am I glad to see you!" Grandma cooed as we
stepped off Old Peg. I was tired. After all, we had traveled
thirteen miles from Stockville to Freedom.

"Come inside, and I'll make you something cool to drink."

"I'll get Old Peg curried off in the barn, and I'll join you,"
Grandpa said.

"Thanks, Granddad," Bob said.

"No problem," he said in return.

So, after being filled up with chocolate-chip cookies and
raspberry Kool-Aid, Bob hopped on Old Peg first, and George
kindly let me step on second.

Name __Erica Wilson__   Date _____

Title __Playin' 'Possum__

Personal Story

	EXCELLENT	GOOD	NEEDS WORK
Focus on One Incident	All the writing focuses on one incident from beginning to end.	Most of the writing focuses on one incident.	The writing never fully describes one incident.
Vocabulary	six or more descriptive words	four or five descriptive words	fewer than four descriptive words
Character, Setting, Problem, Resolution	It is easy to identify characters, setting, problem, and resolution.	The story contains a character, setting, and problem.	The story contains fewer than three story elements.
Varied Sentence Structure	Three or more different sentence structures are used throughout the story.	Two different sentence structures are used.	The same sentence structure is used throughout the story.

▲ *Erica and her peer reader agreed upon this rubric evaluation of her story "Playin' Possum."*

42

Quick-Writes

A quick-write is a simple writing activity with lasting effects. I've found it generates great enthusiasm for story writing, and an unending source of ideas. To prepare for a quick-write, I retype short passages from children's literature that have strong emotional impact. (For grades four through eight, I recommend five to eight sentences.) Next, I photocopy each passage onto an overhead transparency. Before the year begins, I try to make at least eight sets of new quick-writes to add to my supply.

My students enjoyed doing a quick-write using this excerpt from Eve Bunting's novel *SOS Titanic*:

> *There was another terrible bellow as the Titanic blew off more steam. Barry clapped his hands to his ears. He felt as if he were going mad, like Mrs. Cherry Hat. The water had moved up another step. Now it covered his feet, icy cold through his socks and boots. How much would have to come in before it weighed them down? Was the ship about to turn over, belly up?*

I place a passage such as this one on the overhead. I read it aloud twice, using dramatic emphasis. Then I announce that it's time to write. For the next three minutes, my students write nonstop. They may continue with the story line from the quick-write, or they may write anything that pops into their heads. The only rule is: *Don't stop until the three minutes are up.* I also write for three minutes. At the beginning of the year, there might be a hesitant student who can't think of anything to write. In that case, he may simply copy what's on the overhead, but his pencil must keep moving.

Students Share Their Quick-Writes

Then we share. The students love this part. In groups of three or four, they read their pieces to one another. (Make sure you join a group and read your work, too.) If someone wants to share with the whole group, we take time for that, as well. (I usually limit whole-group sharing to three or four students.) More story ideas have come from quick-writes than any other source in the classroom. Many students mark the quick-write pages in their writing workbooks so they can revisit those spots to look for seeds of story ideas.

Why do the children enjoy quick-writes so much? I think there are a few reasons:

- We don't do quick-writes all the time. Once every two weeks is the average, although at the beginning of the year it's more frequent.
- It's a brief exercise, with peer feedback.
- It's fun to hear what others have written.
- It's immediate.
- Since we write quickly, we hear the student's true voice. His or her writing sparkles with wit and personality.

Story Charts That Work

everal years ago, when I first coached teachers on teaching writing, I recommended that every classroom display a large story chart. One such chart looked like this:

CHARACTERS	SETTINGS	PROBLEMS
pirate	forest	can't find way home
mermaid	cave	being chased by dragon
princess	mountains	lost pet
space alien	seashore	tries to rescue a loved one
magician	palace	tries to find a magic potion
queen	cemetery	is kidnapped
alligator	downtown	is afraid of the dark
pioneer child	near a stream	wants a true friend

At that time, I suggested that each student select a character, setting, and problem—for example, *princess, cave,* and *can't find her way home.* I assumed a child would be able to mold a story from these components. Well, I was wrong. I discovered that unless students have a broad background in science fiction or fairy tales involving princesses, mermaids, magicians, or space aliens, they wouldn't know how these characters dressed, traveled, spoke, or behaved. I was asking students to write stories using characters and settings with which they had little or no experience. Their stories were difficult to write and lacked authenticity, clarity, and meaning.

Now I recommend that teachers start with the familiar. Brainstorm with your students, and have them write down all the different types of kids they know at home or school under the heading "Characters." A list from sixth graders might look like this:

CHARACTERS

bully	jock	shy boy
straight-A student	quiet girl	tease
loner	best friend	copycat
competitive girl	know-it-all	artist
show-off	teacher's assistant	comedian
twins	bookworm	nurturer

My experience is that students will easily list 30 to 40 kid characters. Next, ask them for typical settings where children interact. They may say:

Settings

playground	laundromat	ball field
school bathroom	classroom	bus stop
cafeteria	supermarket	backyard
park	movies	bike trails
school bus	the mall	locker room
bleachers	summer camp	library

More settings can be added throughout the year. Let students know that writers are always on the lookout for new characters and settings and often keep notebooks full of their observations. (This board or poster can be considered a giant classroom "notebook.")

Continue the process by including problems from the students' lives. This is the most interesting list of all. Students will offer numerous kinds of problems, such as:

Problems

lousy lunch	losing a friend	not making the team
failing a class	being laughed at	parents getting divorced
brother running away	parent in jail	being bullied
getting wrongful blame	losing the house key	moving to a new school
forced into extracurricular	parents never at home	pet dies
family car wreck	afraid to speak out in class	older sibling too bossy

Sometimes their problems are severe and complex. List everything as they say it. Students can decide later what works well in a story.

The students take every step seriously. Don't be surprised when the chart is brimming over with suggestions. They are so pleased that we, as adults, are finally taking notice of their world and their unique insights into it. And why shouldn't they be their own resource? After all, they are experts: They know the language, dress, conflicts, and feelings of their world better than anyone.

Outfitting the Writer's Toolbox

Idea boards, life stories, quick-writes, and story charts are great springboards for writing, tools that inspire and begin to frame ideas. Once children have chosen a compelling, familiar topic and established a story idea, they are excited about getting started. We want to channel that enthusiasm into strategies that will ensure a well-focused story with a beginning, middle, and end. Next, we will concentrate on the story components themselves. Through our reading, we will give students plenty of practice in identifying and organizing story components, while introducing and modeling another very useful tool: story maps. By understanding what these components are and how they function as critical elements of story structure, students will soon be ready to write strong stories of their own.

Learning Story Structure With Maps

tory maps are graphic organizers that help children recognize the main components of a story. They come in all shapes and sizes. In the early stages of writing development, story maps help students identify the main character, setting, problem, and solution. As the students progress in their reading and writing skills, a more sophisticated story map enables them to single out the three or more episodes that build the conflict of the story.

A fourth grader plans his story. The work students do mapping favorite literature pays off when they go to write their own stories. They have become familiar with the patterns of plot.

Story maps also point out the strengths and weaknesses of the main character and how he or she has grown and changed by the end of the story. Sometimes the character learns he can face a fear and think clearly. Other times, she changes by becoming more accepting or understanding of others. *Students soon learn that a character can only grow if he solves his own problem in the story.*

Story maps require students to pull this information from published stories. As they complete story maps, the components of story writing become firmly planted in their memories for later use, when they are creating their own plans and stories. In fact, you'll find the same kind of information on both story maps and plans.

Model First

As with all the strategies in this book, you need to model the use of the first story map in class, with the students watching and participating. Use picture books for your practice efforts. Since most students will be writing short stories later, it only makes sense to map smaller published works. The focus and plot are easily recognizable in picture books. Middle-grade novels contain subplots and a larger cast of characters—a sophisticated structure that can confuse some students during the initial mapping process.

I suggest starting with simple maps that list the four key story ingredients:

Main Character: _____

Setting: _____

Problem: _____

Solution: _____

As your students' proficiencies increase, you may continue to add story details until you have a map that looks like the one at right (this is my favorite one to use in grades four through eight because the children get a solid view of the structure of the story):

A completed story map might look like this one:

Name _____ Date _____

Story Map

Title and Author: _____
_____

Main Character: _____

Positive Traits: _____ _____ _____

Flaw, Need, or Fear: _____

Setting: _____

Problem (stated in a complete sentence): ____
_____

Episodes: _____
_____
_____
_____

Solution: _____

Character Growth (How did the main character change?): ____
_____
_____

⟨133⟩

Title and Author:
Katie's Trunk by Ann Turner

Main Character: Katie

Positive Traits: fair-minded, thoughtful, spirited

Flaws: strong-willed, sometimes impulsive

Setting: Massachusetts, early 1770s, midday

Problem: Rebels are approaching Katie's home, and she knows they will steal or destroy her family's most treasured possessions.

Episodes:

- Katie gets angry and leaves her hiding place in the woods to defend her home.
- Frightened by the rebels at the front door, Katie hides in Mama's big trunk.
- John Warren, a rebel neighbor, realizes Katie is in the trunk and calls the other marauders away.

Solution: Because of an earlier friendship with her neighbors, the Warrens, Katie's presence prevents the rebels' looting of her home.

Character Growth: Katie learns to balance brave, bold actions with the dangers of the situation. She also appreciates the power of a former friendship between families who are now on opposite sides in a political battle.

Character, Setting, Problem, Episodes

You will need to explain each of the story elements as you show students how to use a story map. In these next few pages, I share with you what I want my children to understand about character, setting, problem, episodes, and character growth. In the course of exploring these elements, my students and I look at books, recall novels and characters we've encountered, make lists, and so on. As a result of these discussions, we become better at filling out story maps, but more importantly, we begin to think about the story characters we want to create in more complex, interesting ways.

Character

Every person has strengths that make him appealing and capable of solving his own problems, but no one is perfect. The same is true with story characters. Students enjoy finding the strong and weak points of a book character. In many well-crafted stories, the problem arises from a flaw, need, fear, or weakness of the main character. We need to guide students to that understanding so that the characters they eventually create will be full and rich.

Positive traits might be:

- lively
- kind
- curious
- imaginative
- intrepid
- helpful
- insightful

Flaws might be:

- forgetful
- worrywart
- impulsive
- brash
- procrastinating
- dishonest
- gossipy
- greedy
- vain
- mistrusting

Flaws: a Crucial Part of a Believable Character

Flaws are innate to the character, while fears and needs arise as the character interacts with external events in the story. Few stories have a character that is plagued by all three. Usually the problem develops because a flaw, need, or fear gets out of control or pushes forward in the story.

For instance, in *Crash* by Jerry Spinelli, seventh grader John ("Crash") Coogan has several strengths. He is aware, intelligent, and athletic. However, he has an important flaw that adds to the tension of the story: He is insecure about his place in his family and in the school community. To overcome this insecurity, he is always trying to get attention through bravado, both in his speech and actions; but as the story progresses, John becomes more secure and his actions change. Growth in character is what drives most solid stories.

Setting

Most students think setting only refers to place. Help them understand that time is a critical part of setting, too. Most of the picture books and short stories that inspire children's writing deal with a very thin slice of time. Sometimes the time period is an afternoon; in other cases, it can be two or three days. Draw the students' attention to the fact that a typical picture book takes one event and magnifies it. Therefore, the time frame is often very short.

Settings might be:

* right before the movie starts on eighth-grade night
* an attic in an old Victorian home after midnight
* the first two days at a new school
* the last art class in sixth grade
* halftime at the junior-varsity football game
* twilight at the beach

The setting in *To Build a Fire* by Jack London is a day in the subzero landscape of Alaska. Amy Littlesugar uses a small southern town and the days preceding the Fourth of July as the setting of *Jonkonnu.* Charles Lindbergh's record-breaking 33-hour transatlantic trip is the setting for *Flight* by Robert Burleigh. Setting subtly drives the plot by stepping up the sense of urgency, danger, or conflict.

Problem

The problem in a story is usually something the main character wants or needs, but doesn't have, or can't do. Often this directly refers back to a personal weakness or flaw of the main character. Help students identify the problem in as few words as possible. For example: "Because Mary Lou is impulsive and bold, she blurts out private information about her best friend and loses that friend." The rest of the story can be about Mary Lou's struggle to rebuild her friend's trust in her.

The problem leads to the struggle depicted in the episodes. It is critical to stress to children that without a problem, there is no story. There might be a list of events, a concept, or a description, but no story. Quite often this is what weakens students' first stories. Many want to list several events from a vacation or a party. Let them know that a story always focuses on a central problem that worsens as the story proceeds.

Problems might be:

- Kyle hears a strange sound coming from the basement but can't find its source.
- The history club tries to save the old bridge as a landmark, but developers want to tear it down.
- Laura needs to rescue her dog or he will be swept into the rapids and die.
- Marie, the lead in the eighth-grade play, is failing math and won't be allowed to perform unless she gets a B on the next test.

Episodes

The episodes form the middle of the story. These are the attempts to solve the problem (or conflict). Additionally, the tension of the story usually grows with each episode. In most picture books and short stories, there are three main episodes in the middle of the story (this varies, but three is the norm). This middle of the story is called either the struggle or the conflict and it is where the main character works hard to solve the problem.

Since most students have trouble recognizing the episodes of plot development, take extra time to explore it. Ask them to begin with common problems in their own lives. For example: How would you convince your parents to let you do something they strongly oppose? If your pet were lost, how would you go about finding it? What would you do if your best friend moved away? If you got caught doing something wrong, how would you regain your parents' trust? Brainstorm all possible solutions then ask: *Would that work? Why? What might go wrong?*

As you talk about literature with students, frame your questions so that they amplify the notion that a main character is always striving to solve something. For example:

- Where did Kyle look? What did he find?
- What did they do to save the bridge? Did it work? Why?
- What did Laura do to try to save her dog? Did it work? Why or why not?
- What did Marie do to learn the math? Did it work? Why or why not?

From time to time, ask students to brainstorm different ways of resolving a character's main problem. Then discuss whether these alternatives would work in light of the character's personality traits. This type of discussion helps children see the interrelationship between character and plot more clearly.

Growth of Character

The resolution of a problem is not really the most important outcome of a story. What's emotionally satisfying for a reader is that by the story's end, the main character has usually grown and changed in some significant way. After reading a story, you might ask these types of questions to nudge students toward that discovery:

- How did the character change from the beginning of the story to the end?
- Would the character at the end of the story act the same way now in a similar situation?
- Is the character braver than before? more inventive? less fearful? more resourceful? Did he or she discover one of life's truths?

In addition, help students understand these aspects of episodic character development:

- There are good and bad events throughout the plot.
- No real problem is solved with the first attempt.
- The main character perseveres until the end.
- No outside force, such as parents, teachers, best friends, or magic, solves the problem for the main character.
- The main character changes for the better by the end of the story.

Vary Story Genres and Mapping Strategies

One collaborative use of a story map is not enough; only repeated practice with it will solidify story structure for your students. Concurrently, you must vary the types of stories you use with the class. Fifteen mysteries will only help your students become comfortable with mapping that specific genre. Explore a blend of historical fiction, tales, realistic fiction, fantasy, humor, adventure, and nature stories.

Story Charts

At the beginning of the year, it is helpful to devote an entire bulletin board to a story chart, where students classify stories and their elements from your read-aloud picture books, short stories, and novels. This is a marvelous form of visual support for your students as they delve into story structure. You might even place this out in the hall and invite other classrooms to add their stories to the chart. I'm always amazed how much more involved students become in an activity when peers from another classroom join in and respond.

TITLE/AUTHOR	GENRE	MAIN CHARACTER	FLAW, NEED, OR FEAR	SETTING
The Ice Horse by Candace Christiansen	historical fiction	Jack, a 12-year-old boy	needs to prove he is responsible	Hudson River, New York, 1920s
The Fortune-Tellers by Lloyd Alexander	humorous tale	a young carpenter	needs to know his future	West African village, any year
So Far From the Sea by Eve Bunting	realistic fiction	Laura Iwasaki	needs to say good-bye to her grandfather at his grave	Manzanar War Relocation Camp in California, 1972
The Memory Coat by Elvira Woodruff	historical fiction	Rachel, a Jewish girl	fears that her family will be harmed or separated	Russia, early 1900s
Thank You, Mr. Falker by Patricia Polacco	autobiographical tale	Trisha, a struggling reader	fears being teased by classmates	classrooms, grades 1–5, mid-1900s
Maple Moon by Connie Brummel Cook	Native-American tale	crippled Missisauga boy named "Rides the Wind"	needs to prove his value to the tribe	a long time ago, great forest in Canada

"Illustrative Style" in this chart refers to the medium and technique used by the illustrator to enhance a story's meaning through visual imagery. Students quickly become able to distinguish pen-and-ink drawings from watercolors, pastels from colored pencil and woodcuts, and so on. Discussion of these artistic considerations will give them ideas of what medium to select when illustrating a story of their own later on.

PROBLEM	SOLUTION	CHARACTER'S GROWTH	ILLUSTRATIVE STYLE
Jack must listen and work hard to learn a job that will help Uncle Joe harvest ice on the river.	Jack learns to rely on himself and is able to help, even in the worst of times.	Jack is proud of the job he has done and knows he has gained Uncle Joe's respect.	oil paints/realistic
The carpenter must tell the fortunes of others who believe he can see into the future.	He learns to tell good fortunes and make everyone happy.	realizes there isn't much talent or art needed to be a fortune-teller	ink, acrylic, and crayon
Laura doesn't want to move to Boston without a special farewell to her grandfather.	Laura leaves a symbol of her father's and grandfather's love of America.	Laura creates a fitting memorial that pleases herself and her family.	watercolor
Rachel and her family must flee Russia and enter America through Ellis Island.	Rachel creatively helps her family pass by the inspectors at Ellis Island.	Rachel knows that her cleverness contributed to her family's safety.	oil on canvas
Trisha struggles with reading and math—everything is jumbled and confusing.	Trisha works hard after school with Mr. Falker and a reading teacher.	Trisha learns that she can learn to read, step by step, day by day. She gains confidence.	Pentel markers, acrylics, oil pastels
Rides the Wind wants to find a way he can contribute to his tribe during a hard winter.	Rides the Wind convinces the unbelieving tribe that he has found the source of sweet sap.	Rides the Wind gains confidence in himself and respect among the tribe.	oil on canvas

Keep Building the Framework

With repeated use of summaries, story charts, main dramatic questions, and story maps, your students' understanding of story writing will continue to grow. It is critical that you provide this practice before asking them to create their own stories. When this support is in place and they have a healthy supply of ideas, it is time to let them experiment with their own writing. In fact, be forewarned: By now they'll likely be begging for opportunities to write their own stories!

Bringing Characters to Life

Published fiction writers spend a great amount of time getting to know their characters. Some draw sketches of their main characters and hang them up in their offices for months. They have conversations with these fictional characters. They list attributes beneath and around the pictures. Sometimes they write letters to these "people" to learn

Seventh grader Matt Nickel works on a character sketch for his story "Brett West."

more about them, and the characters write them letters back. Sometimes they imagine these characters in different situations and decide their actions. They list their characters' likes, dislikes, fears, and needs until three-dimensional people emerge.

These writers know that character development is fundamental to writing a good story. Jean Karl, an editor of children's books for more than forty years, points out the value of creating a believable character in her book *How to Write and Sell Children's Picture Books* (Writer's Digest Books, 1994):

> How do characters become real? They become real when they are real to you. They become real when you know them so well that you know how they talk, how they react to not only the situations in your story, but to most events of their daily lives, when you know both their good points and their bad points.... As you think about your characters, write down words that describe them, make lists of words that describe how they move, words that might be a part of their speech, words that might exemplify the way they think.

When I develop characters with students, I follow her advice. Just as "character" is always listed first on a story map or a story plan, creating a strong character is the critical first step in story writing.

Model Lesson: Creating a Character

I've divided this lesson into three parts. I try to do all of it in one marathon session, but if you need to do it over a couple of days, you'll find your own natural places to pause the lesson. Here's how I would begin the lesson at the overhead:

Character Sketch

I begin by thinking out loud:

Since I want this story to be about a child in middle school, I need to pick an age first. I'll choose a sixth grader, a twelve-year-old. Next, I need to decide if it's going to be a girl or a boy. I want this character to be a boy.

[On the overhead, I write]:

boy—12—6th grade

Now I begin asking myself questions about this character so I can get to know him. I write my brief answers down the page. The questions touch on personal characteristics, family information, information about school and friends, likes and dislikes, positive traits, fears, flaws, needs, and desires. The students listen and watch as I create this character:

Does he have brothers or sisters?

one brother, 18 years old

Does he live with a mom and a dad?

lives with mom—parents divorced

Does he have a pet?

dog—German Shepherd

Does he live in the city or the country?

lives in suburb

What does he like to do in his spare time?

shoot baskets whenever and wherever he can

What's under his bed?

basketball trading cards and empty candy wrappers

Does he have his own bedroom?

yes

What's his favorite meal?

meatballs and macaroni and cheese

Where's his favorite place to go and be alone?

sits on a large rock down by a creek

What color is his hair?

brown

Is it long or short?

very short

What does he usually wear?

khaki shorts, T-shirt, and running shoes

What is something he always does around the house to be helpful?

keeps the garage clean and empties all the trash twice a week

What's his favorite phrase to say when he's angry?

"Leave me alone. Now!"

Who is his best friend in his neighborhood?

Mandy—the girl next-door

What do they like to do together?

watch NBA Showtime and dig worms for fishing

What is he afraid of the most?

not being liked at school or not being on the school basketball team

Are there any animals that scare him?

big snakes and large, angry dogs

What's his personality flaw?

procrastinates about doing homework

What are two good traits he has?

friendly toward everyone and helpful to others

What kinds of things upset him?

any kind of bigotry and girls who are always calling boys on the telephone

What did he do last that got him into trouble at home?

sneaked out on a school night to go to a basketball exhibition game with friends

What were the consequences?

grounded from all evening activities for three weeks

What does he like best about his brother?

he can drive, so they can go and do things away from the house together

What does he like best about his mom?

she doesn't yell or cry a lot—she is usually in a good mood

How does he get to school?

rides school bus

What kind of student is he?

bright—but hates studying, homework, and tests

What do his teachers think of him?

that he's polite but could work harder

What's his best subject?

science—good at "hands-on" and coming up with conclusions

What's his worse subject?

math—understands it—but doesn't do all the homework and never wants to study it

What does he like best about school?

being one of the forwards on the basketball team

What does he like least about school?

taking tests—especially math tests

How do the other students feel about him?

they like him a lot—he's helpful and an all-around great friend

What did he do the last time he got in trouble at school?

didn't turn in his homework in math class for one full week

What were the consequences?

received five F's that week, which dropped his average to a D

Has he ever won any awards at school?

in sixth grade, won an art award for sculpture; in fifth grade, won a spelling bee; in fourth grade, won first place in the school art contest

Does he ever get to see his father?

sees his dad one weekend a month, plus his dad comes to all his basketball games and takes him to dinner one night a week

What one thing would he like to be better at than he is?

making free throws

What piece of clothing does he wear everyday?

a Pacer's hat

What do he and his friends do when they see each other at school?

nod and say, "What's up?"

Does he have a nickname?

"Dunk," because he sinks a lot of baskets each game for his team

What's his favorite movie?

Hoosiers

If he could change one thing about himself what would it be?

would like to be three inches taller

How tall is he?

5'8"

What helps him in school?

easily understands most new things

I try to ask 30–40 questions. The trick is to keep a balance between simple questions about likes and dislikes and more penetrating ones about fears or needs. You want to make sure that each writer examines the character in depth. If the list only reflects likes and dislikes, there will not be enough material to build a story. That said, it's important to tell students that most of the information in the character sketch will never find its way into their stories. We create a well-defined character so that we will know what this character will do and say in the story. Each piece of information fleshes out the character more fully in the writer's mind.

PART 2

Making Up a Name

Now I model the process of thinking up an original name for my character. I let students know that I want a name that readers will remember. Sometimes the personality profile dictates a name. For example, since the character we've outlined above is friendly, basketball-loving, and a procrastinator when it comes to homework, I say to the students, "When I think of the qualities of my character, no particular name seems suited to him unless I use his nickname and combine that with a last name. My character could have a name of Brad McGuire, but maybe the kids call him 'Dunk' McGuire."

PART 3

Identifying the Problem

After generating a list of preferences and behaviors and choosing a name for my character, it's time to find a story problem. While modeling, I go back over the profile and, in color, circle any possible sources of conflict. I circle the character's fears, flaws, needs, wishes—anything that suggests a less-than-comfortable picture. In this character profile, I would circle:

What is he afraid of the most?

not being liked at school or not being on the school basketball team

Are there any animals that scare him?

big snakes and large, angry dogs

What's his personality flaw?

procrastinates about doing homework*

I love spending time with students discussing the distinctive names in the books we read. Together we notice that Kevin Henkes uses one-of-a-kind names like Chrysanthemum, Owen, or Chester to capture the personality of his characters. Other authors choose names that match outstanding traits of their characters. In *Cut-ups*, James Marshall named his two bungling heroes Spud and Joe—perfect names for these two mischievous characters. We discuss the names Summer, Ob, and Cletus from Cynthia Rylant's *Missing May*, and Fern from *Charlotte's Web*. I also explain the use of nicknames to capture the talents or personality of a character.

Come prepared to such a discussion. Have some unusual names from literature or your imagination ready to share with them. Ask them to design personalities that would complement the names. Students enjoy this exercise. It also makes them aware of perfectly chosen names in the stories they read. Your class might even decide to create a name board in the classroom. As students hear, read, or see unusual names, they can add them to the collection.

What kinds of things upset him?

any kind of bigotry and girls who are always calling boys on the telephone

What did he do last that got him into trouble at home?

sneaked out on a school night to go to a basketball exhibition game with friends

What kind of student is he?

bright—but hates studying, homework, and tests

What's his worse subject?

math—understands it—but doesn't do all the homework and never wants to study it

What does he like least about school?

taking tests—especially math tests

What did he do the last time he got in trouble at school?

didn't turn in his homework in math class for one full week

What were the consequences?

received five F's that week, which dropped his average to a D

If he could change one thing about himself what would it be?

would like to be three inches taller

Students Jump In

As you are developing your character on the overhead, don't be surprised if the students offer answers to questions you raise. Students quickly become involved in the process, excitedly watching the character come to life right before their eyes. Some children will begin to draw your character on paper as your description grows. Encourage their participation; but if you have sound reasoning as to why one answer is better than another, explain this reasoning to your students.

Now the students and I look for areas of importance in our character's life. With Brad "Dunk" McGuire, this seems obvious: Dunk likes anything and everything that has to do with basketball, especially *playing* basketball. To create a problem, we think of something that might interfere with him playing basketball.

As we've discovered from looking at literature, most problems place the main character in a position where she wants or needs something that is initially out of reach but ultimately attainable. If the goal is unattainable, you don't have a realistic story, because either magic or a miracle is needed to reach that goal.

I remind students that a story needs a hero or heroine who is struggling to achieve an end. It's the struggle—the events that make the story hang together—that creates the conflict. True conflict always has a little good and a little bad mixed up in it. A story with all good events would be monotonous: How many of us teachers have read cheerful but dull vacation "stories" recapping only the happy moments? A story filled with one bad event after another is boring, too, and leaves the reader discouraged and overwhelmed.

For our story, we need to identify a problem that Dunk can overcome, one that will offer him a struggle along the way. Resolving this problem will enable Dunk to have or do something he otherwise would not have or could not do. I now ask the students:

What could keep Dunk McGuire from playing basketball? Hmmm, let's see. One of the flaws we circled showed Dunk sneaking out on a school night and getting grounded. So that's a possibility: Disobeying the rules of his home could interfere with his basketball. Another flaw we circled was Dunk's procrastination about work and how he hates to study for or take tests. Since this is mentioned more than once, I think we should use it as the source of the problem.

Once we identify strong patterns in a personality profile, the problem just seems to pop out. On the overhead, I write these two significant pieces of information:

Dunk lives and breathes basketball. It is important to Dunk that he plays on the school team.

Dunk sometimes procrastinates when he's supposed to be studying. Also, he doesn't like tests, especially math tests.

I leave a large space on the overhead between these two statements and begin brainstorming ways to connect them in a problem. I then write down the connections we come up with and comment aloud on how well each one might work.

Dunk lives and breathes basketball. It is important to Dunk that he plays on the school team.

STORY PROBLEM	VIABILITY
✱ Dunk fails math test and is taken off the team.	*difficult to solve*
✱ Dunk puts off studying for math test until the night before.	*provides tension and could be solved by Dunk*
✱ Dunk keeps procrastinating on his math homework until he is so far behind that his grade falls too low and he is taken off the basketball team.	*again, difficult to solve*
✱ Dunk's procrastination spreads to his other classes, and all his grades begin to drop. He could be placed on academic probation and lose his spot on the team.	*provides tension and could be solved by Dunk*

Dunk sometimes procrastinates when he's supposed to be studying. Also, he doesn't like tests, especially math tests.

Afterward, I tell the class that I am selecting the second choice, because the story could be tightly focused on a small period of time and one particular class. This would enable me to keep the tension high.

Using Brad "Dunk" McGuire's strong and weak points, I construct a tentative problem for the story:

Dunk procrastinates about studying for a big math test and waits until the night before. If he gets another poor grade, he will be removed from the basketball team for the rest of the season.

Have Students Create Their Own Characters

I suggest collaborating with students on this activity a couple more times before you have them work independently. They won't need too much practice in answering questions about imagined characters; however, they *will* need practice in identifying their characters' weaknesses, flaws, needs, and fears and turning them into story problems.

When the students are ready to create their own characters, I support them in a different manner. First, I prompt them with questions. These can be the same questions I used when creating my character profile of Dunk McGuire. Then, when they have a completed profile and a character name, they work in groups of four. Each student introduces his/her character by name and shares five critical pieces of information about that character. The other three members ask the student questions for three minutes. These are new questions, not ones we have addressed during the earlier character-development activity. For example, they might ask:

* ✿ How would this character react if someone stole his lunch money?
* ✿ What does your character do when she doesn't understand a school assignment?
* ✿ When was the last time your character raised his voice? Why?
* ✿ Would you be good friends with your character?
* ✿ What is your character's favorite book?

The writer has the opportunity to both ask and field questions. The only rule is that he must respond as quickly as possible to others' questions, relying on his instincts to

Story Frame

Main Character: Nick

Three good traits:
1. good at math
2. has a horse and a cat
3. he's gentle and kind

A flaw, a need, a desire, or a weakness
fear of girls and spiders
Setting: Place live specimen museum
Time after closing

Problem: (one sentence)
Nick is trapped with three whining, crying girls in an animal museum.

Events: (conflicts, struggle, episodes)
1. Nick and girls are ready to go back - But they're lost in the museum Nick runs & checks doors - checks big map
2. Nick & girls find front door - locked lights go out, girls panic & cuddle up to Nick
Nick tells them, "Get away!"

3. sounds - lightning, thunder
shadows
girls crying, whining
expecting Nick to help them

Solution: Nick has to devise a way (sensors) and comforts girls

▲ *A fourth grade's collaborative story plan.*

formulate the answers and make them consistent with the profile. This forces students to think more deeply about the characters they've created and to get to know them better. It also pushes them to revise their profiles, eliminating any inconsistencies that emerge.

Encourage the students in the group to pause while the writer makes revisions in her sketch. For instance, if she originally notes that the character is resourceful but later says he asks his parents to do everything for him, she needs to address this contradiction. Sometimes, the listeners point out these slips to the writer; other times, the writer herself catches the conflicting statements when she reads her sketch aloud.

The following character sketch was developed by a student:

"Brett West"
by Matt Nickel, grade 7

age 15

male

lives with stepdad and mother—visits father and stepmother

has a half-sister, stepsister, and brother

his home looks like the Home Alone house in the movies

house is usually dark—boring but scary, too—things have happened**

he is rich

getaway, goes to an old, abandoned grocery store**

pleases everyone at home by being energetic and happy

last time in trouble, was with friends he wasn't supposed to be with

got blamed for smoking when it was stepbrother**

has wavy black hair that is dyed blonde

left ear is pierced

has a baggy, "limpy" walk—left foot is messed up

very polite around adults

inline skates on ramps and such

has several friends from all over town

most of his friends are not much like him

has a fear of falling through ice and not being able to get back up

is kind, funny, and has stamina for aggressive sports

weakness is, is still not totally mature—very irresponsible**

school: good at drama—always acting and making voices

wants to be like Robin Williams

not too organized, doesn't have a great reputation with teachers**

had problems at other schools

twice suspended for stupid things like graffiti and fighting**

** indicates the areas of concern that could develop into a problem

---

Matt chose this for his problem: *Immature behavior leads Brett to fall through the ice while skating with friends.*

Three Days of Lessons

Have students work on character development over a period of three days. On day one, students can answer the first group of questions you ask to help them create profiles. On the second day, they can name their characters, share information about them, and answer questions from peers in a small-group setting. The third day, they can meet again in the same small groups to identify possible areas of conflict and come up with workable problems.

Let Students Invent Characters by Drawing Them

Depending on the circumstances, I have given my students an opportunity to draw their characters before or after they create a character profile. For many, completing the art beforehand is a must. As they draw, their minds are actively composing the personalities of these characters. For others, sketching their character in words and thoughts comes first. After you know your students well enough, add this dimension as you see fit. Unfortunately, I find it difficult to draw anything but stick figures. So I never draw my characters, but I have had students bring my characters to life on the overhead or blackboard.

Character is Everything

Many professional writers will tell you that character is everything—get it right, and the rest of the story takes care of itself. To solidify students' understanding of character development and prepare them for story writing, try sketching four to six characters collaboratively early on in the year. Use the believable tensions and conflicts that emerge from these character sketches to construct a central story problem. Once that problem is known, the next step is the story plan.

Constructing Story Plans

A fourth grader uses the posted class plan to help him organize his own story.

So far we have discussed ways of developing story ideas and how to create believable characters and story problems. Now we are ready to explore two other considerations that need to be defined in order to build a good story: purpose and audience.

Purpose

Let's say a student wants to write a story about her dog running away from home and unexpectedly returning five weeks later. If the purpose is to entertain, she may choose to use the voice of the dog or perhaps the family cat, who's happy Fido is on the lam. If she wants to write a serious story that focuses on her fears that the dog is lost forever, then she might write it from her own point of view.

Her purpose will determine the style, tone, point of view, and focus of the piece. If she chooses the first example, the story will most likely have playful, maybe even mischievous, language and scenes; ideas of freedom and discovery will engage the reader. If she goes with the second, the story will have a more somber tone and suspense, and tenderness will be used to draw us in. Therefore, the author has to make this important decision before continuing with a plan. Once she has made that choice, her next decision involves her story's audience.

Audience

If the story has an anticipated audience of nine- to fourteen-year-olds, then vocabulary and sentence structure can be more sophisticated. The author will be able to relate her feelings to others in her age group with appropriate detail. If the story is written for younger students, five- to eight-year-olds, the author will need to keep the text brief. Her story will have to use simpler language and sentence construction. Illustrations will be needed to convey some of the story's meaning. These are generalizations, but each story requires some individual thought and adjustments to its presentation.

Compare and Contrast Authors' Purposes and Intended Audiences

As a class, compare the picture books of Eric Carle, Audrey and Don Wood, Harriet Ziefert, or Bill Martin, Jr. with the more sophisticated stories of Deborah Hopkinson, Roald Dahl, Rafe Martin, or David Wisniewski. Identify these authors' purposes and the audiences they are writing for.

Use the following considerations when comparing story audience:

- subject or content
- amount of text per page
- amount of description
- use of literary devices (such as simile, metaphor, flashback, and foreshadowing)
- detail of illustrations
- sentence structure
- sentence length
- vocabulary choice
- print size
- title
- cover art

Examples of purpose and intended audience in published books are:

Ada's Pal by George Ella Lyon

AUDIENCE: ages 4–8
PURPOSE: to show how families and friends grieve, cope, and accept a death

More Than Anything Else by Marie Bradby

AUDIENCE: ages 4–10
PURPOSE: to reveal a dream of literacy that Booker T. Washington held in his heart at age nine

Golem by David Wisniewski

AUDIENCE: ages 9–12
PURPOSE: to explain the legend of Golem the giant, made of clay by Rabbi Loew to protect the Jews of Prague

After a thorough explanation and demonstration of purpose and audience, you'll need only an occasional reminder for children to incorporate both into their prewriting plans. To support them further, encourage them to add the entries "Purpose" and "Audience" to their story plans. These can be written on the top or on the back of the plan. (Some students like to write brief summaries and main dramatic questions for their stories on the back of story plans, as well. Keeping all of these notations in one place prevents wasted time searching for small scraps of paper in a desk or file.)

Take note that for some writers, both novice and veteran, purpose and audience can change as the story unfolds. Despite all of our organizational tools, the human spirit will continue to discover the true story as it is written. Be open to this change, and let students learn for themselves that this, too, is part of the writing process.

Possible Purposes for Student Story Writing

- to explain something in nature (myth or "just so" story)
- to entertain with humor
- to relate a personal story
- to share an incident from family history
- to show a slice of history from a child's point of view (historical fiction)
- to introduce scientific information within the context of a story
- to demonstrate one of life's truths (fable)
- to stretch the limits of the natural world (science fiction)
- to write an original tale
- to offer a different version of a traditional tale (retold tale)
- to share a mystery or story of suspense
- to write a survival story
- to explain a legend
- to provide insight into a famous person's actions

Possible Audiences for Student Story Writing

- preschool children
- primary-grade children
- peers/friends
- children in intermediate grades
- parents and family
- grandparents
- the general public

Story Plans

Every good story needs a plan. Without one, a story tends to meander, lose focus, and fall flat. So after students have chosen a story idea, selected a purpose, and identified their intended audience, they are ready to build an organized framework for their story.

I don't mince words with students. I tell them right off, "I expect all of you to put a lot of work into your plans. I hope you become frustrated with episodes that don't work. I hope you struggle with appropriate endings. If you go through that strenuous problem-solving now, you will find that writing the story is the fun part. From that point on, you will have a workable story that you know well and like. The writing will simply jazz it up, adding detail and interesting vocabulary that make it enjoyable for you and the reader."

Many teachers know the angst of helping students write stories for days on end, sometimes weeks. There are the usual interruptions with holidays, assemblies, class trips, and so on. Story writing seems to drag on and on. Students lose enthusiasm, and so do we. We get caught up in conferencing and revision and more conferencing, and pretty soon we just want these stories to be *done*.

One of the rewards of helping students craft thorough plans is that the actual writing of the first draft usually ends up taking only 45 to 75 minutes. They can write like the wind when they know where their stories are going, and they're thrilled. Students have told me:

> *"Having a story plan helped dramatically in the actual writing of the story. When you have a plan, you don't have to keep track of what's going to happen next, it's all right there. You just have to add the details."*

> *"It's work—hard work. It took me three days to finally get a plan I knew would tell the story I wanted to write."*

> *"The hardest part for me is thinking about the episodes. They need to build the conflict or tension. Sometimes it takes me a long time to be able to do this, but I'm getting better."*

> *"I don't have as much trouble now finding a resolution to a problem. It seems like it just comes naturally out of my episodes."*

An eighth grader plans her story. ▶

Model Lesson: Writing a Story Plan

always put an empty plan on the overhead so all students can watch me work. The great thing about story plans is that they look the same as story maps. The only difference is now the writer's imagination gets to decide what to write.

Name _____ Date _____

Story Plan

Main Character: _____

Strengths: _____

_____

Flaw, Need, or Fear:_____

Setting: **where** _____ **when** _____

Problem (stated in a complete sentence): _____

_____

Episodes:　**1.** (external action) _____

　　　　　　　(internal action) _____

　　　　　　2. (external action) _____

　　　　　　　(internal action) _____

　　　　　　3. (external action)_____

　　　　　　　(internal action) _____

Resolution: _____

Character Growth: _____

_____

(134)

Teaching Narrative Writing: The Tools That Work for Every Student　Scholastic Professional Books

Defining the Problem

If I'm working in a sixth-grade classroom, I select an eleven- or twelve-year-old character so that students can relate. Ideally, I would already have a character sketch developed. The more interconnected our modeling is, the more easily students understand the process. The following story plan uses Brad "Dunk" McGuire from Chapter 6:

Main character: Brad (also known as "Dunk"), a 12-year-old boy

Strengths: friendly, athletic, and helpful to other students

I tell the students, "I'm not sure these strengths will help Brad later with his problem. I might have to return to these and change one or two. I'll see."

Flaw: procrastinates

I try to pick a flaw that can lend itself to a lot of different problems at this age. I remind the students that we had established a problem at the end of our character sketch.

Setting: **where**—in sixth-grade math class

　　　　　　　　when—right before the end of semester

I'm starting now to have a problem form in my mind. I added "right before the end of semester" to put extra pressure on the main character—to heighten tension right from the beginning of the story.

Problem: At this point, I brainstorm a number of problems in front of the students. If I'm working in a room in which characters, settings, and problems have been listed, I try out different problems from that list and see if they work. If I'm working from an established character sketch, I have a set direction. I might say:

1   *Dunk has known for a month that a big, final math project, worth 40% of the grade, is due on January 4, the next day, but he has procrastinated and not even yet begun.* I like this problem. It is lifelike and has probably happened to many students. My one main concern with it is that I don't know how he could really do a thorough job and still earn a good grade at this late date. It might be hard to have the main character solve this problem and grow as a result. I'll try another idea.

2   *The big, end-of-semester math test is tomorrow, and Dunk has put off studying, so he is not ready to earn a good grade; and if his grade falls beneath a "C," he's off the basketball team.* I like this problem because it could really happen, and no one can help Dunk out of this fix but himself. On the other hand, he might have some friends who could help him, since one of his strengths is that he has helped other students in the past. I'll see what other problems I can create.

3   *Dunk's friend Lucas, the star forward on the basketball team, needs help studying to pass the big, end-of-semester test. He has asked Dunk, but Dunk has put off cleaning the locker rooms for the coach, and tonight is the last night he can do it if he wants to start in the first game.* I really like this problem, because Dunk will have to give up something personal for the good of the team and to help his friend. It gives me an opportunity to show the character growth of Dunk as the story unwinds. Let's see if I can come up with another problem.

4   *Dunk and his basketball rival, Allen, have both put off studying for the end-of-semester final in math class, and if only one passes, that person will be the starting forward in the first game.* Again, I think this problem has strong potential to develop into a good plot. Dunk has gotten himself into this predicament, but since he helps other students, it will be hard for him to turn his back on Allen.

Even though I like the double opportunity for growth in this last problem, I think I'll stick to the simplest problem (which focuses totally on Dunk). Therefore, the best choice is number two, but I think I'll modify it a little to make it more realistic.

Problem: Dunk has put off studying math for weeks, and if his end-of-semester test grade falls beneath a "C," he has to sit on the bench for the first three basketball games.

Determining Episodes

Okay, now we're ready to string together the story's episodes. Episodic development has two threads, *internal* and *external*. The main character responds to the changes around himself or herself with both personal feelings and actions. Older students are capable of understanding that this duality adds depth and a lifelike quality to their stories.

To reinforce the concepts of external and internal action, talk through some real-life episodes with your students. Ask them what they'd do if a parent were to deny them a privilege they were hoping to get. Then ask them how they'd feel and how they'd show those feelings. Second, ask how they'd react if a strange dog were to chase them. Then ask them how they would feel and how they would show those feelings. After a few examples like these, students will begin to think about both behaviors when describing their scenes.

Here's what I write on the overhead:

EPISODES: 1. (external) After class, Dunk's teacher reminds him about the importance of the test.

(internal) Dunk is worried—looks at what he needs to review, but doesn't want to miss out on basketball—it's his favorite.

2. (external) After school, Dunk's buddies ask him to join them for a basketball party and to shoot hoops.

(internal) When he explains, his teammates tease him (somewhat angrily)—he feels left out like he let the team down, since he let his math go.

3. (external) Dunk asks the teacher for help—answer is no, too busy.

(internal) He is overwhelmed—then remembers basketball advice he gives others when they're having a bad practice or game.

As the students watch you work through these episodes, they'll get excited about helping you change your ideas. Let them join in. This is how they learn to problem-solve through the sticky parts. During this process, you'll be trying out different things and erasing along the way. Sometimes you'll get down to episode three and realize you want the story to begin differently. Great! We want the students to see you working hard at this, deciding how to make it all fit together.

Understand that the first few times you do this, it will take you an hour or so. It's worth the investment of time. Your modeling is laying a great foundation. Don't worry: The kids will stay with you and offer suggestions along the way. Something I've learned from working through story plans in many different classrooms is that it's usually the children who are struggling in reading or writing who contribute the most during these think-aloud sessions.

What We've Learned

After working with a variety of teachers on story plans, we have come to some conclusions:

- It's essential for the teacher to model this process at least three times in front of students.

- The class needs to work collaboratively at least five times in creating a workable story plan.

- These experiences build a wonderful background for later critique groups. If a class learns story development together, they share a common language and understanding that will enhance their comments during small-group critiques.

Creating Workable Solutions

Now we're ready to map out the *resolution*. Students need to hear you say, "The main character must solve his own problem. Parents, teachers, or friends don't come in and save the day in a well-written story. The character must do it himself—through courage, ingenuity, inventiveness, perseverance, endurance, or whatever personal strengths he possesses. His personal characteristics help him solve the story's main conflict." In this story, I would say, "It would be easy for Dunk to ask his teammates for help, but that would be too pat of an ending. He needs to work toward this character test. He needs to sacrifice and see what the outcome is."

It's also important for students to realize that when creating endings, a writer wants to avoid making things too nice and tidy. Life isn't always neat and perfect. The character whose father returns won't be happy forever. The character who shows amazing endurance when carrying his injured brother three miles downriver won't remain the strongest boy forever.

Characters, like people, show growth in spurts. They gain experience and wisdom day by day. Weak endings tend to preach or state absolutes, or explain that it was all a dream. They can ruin an otherwise strong and engaging story.

For this story that I am creating about Dunk, I need to formulate the basketball advice he has given to his teammates in the past. This will enable me to write an authentic ending that matches his temperament.

If the advice was, "When the going gets tough, the tough get going," then having Dunk lock himself in the bedroom and work through the night reviewing each math section again and again is one suitable ending. It's a "tough" approach to the problem.

If the advice was, "You've done it before, you'll do it again. Be patient," then Dunk may gain enough self-confidence to realize that he knew most of this math at one time. Therefore, instead of rereading every single page, he might pinpoint a few problems at the back of each chapter and find out what he really needs to study to feel well prepared. This approach might be a more orderly, less-stressful review.

If the advice was, "What you expect is what you get," then maybe Dunk will study with the expectation that he will do well tomorrow because he likes math, understands math, and knows that he can do it.

Many students may feel it's necessary to play out this story all the way to the end of the test, but, as readers and writers become sensitive to story construction, they'll realize that the problem is in fact resolved when Dunk has a plan of attack for the test. It will not be necessary to present a scene in which he gets his test back with a large B+ at the top. Instead, look for a way to end the story with the self-confidence that he gets from his own advice. For instance:

Resolution: Dunk recites to himself, "What you expect is what you get." He studies like a winner, and the next day takes the test with confidence.

Character Growth: Dunk places the same confidence in himself that he instills in his friends when they are feeling less than capable.

Now let's look at the entire story plan and see if anything needs to be changed before we write.

Main Character: "Dunk" (whose real name is Brad), a twelve-year-old boy

Strengths: friendly, athletic, and helpful to other students

Flaw, Fear, or Need: procrastinates

Setting: where—in sixth-grade math class

when—right before the end of semester

Problem: Dunk has put off studying math for weeks, and if his end-of-semester test grade falls beneath a "C," he has to sit on the bench for the first three basketball games.

EPISODES: 1. (external)   After class, Dunk's teacher reminds him about the importance of the test.

(internal)   Dunk is worried—looks at what he needs to review, but doesn't want to miss out on basketball—it's his favorite.

2. (external)   After school, Dunk's buddies ask him to join them for a basketball party and to shoot hoops.

(internal)   When he explains, his teammates tease him (somewhat angrily)—he feels left out like he let the team down, since he let his math go.

3. (external)   Dunk asks the teacher for help—answer is no, too busy.

(internal)   He is overwhelmed—then remembers basketball advice he gives others when they're having a bad practice or game.

Resolution: Dunk recites to himself, "What you expect is what you get." He studies like a winner, and the next day takes the test with confidence.

Character Growth: Dunk places the same confidence in himself that he instills in his friends when they are feeling less than capable.

After rereading this plan, I might want to "tweak" the ending. I said that two of Brad's strengths are that he is *friendly* and *helpful to other students*. Therefore, maybe he passes another player on the team as he's leaving school. This team member might remind Brad of his own advice and how it helped this boy a few months ago. As Brad's walking home, he might begin to repeat this advice and see how it applies to himself. That way, a friend can remind Brad of his own wise words, but it is still Brad who has to put them into action.

Brad's three strengths shine as attributes that help him overcome his own problem. The setting gives an urgency to the problem. There is a small window of time to resolve the problem. The problem seems realistic for a sixth-grade boy. The series of episodes could really take place. Nothing seems contrived—it's a workable plan. We want to model the problem-solving that is needed to create a story plan often, and then work collaboratively with the class until students have the skills to assemble a workable plan. Our goal, though, is to have students eventually create their own story plans. We could make it our goal to intervene and check each one of their plans ourselves to ensure later success. But I prefer to place responsibility on their shoulders. One way to help them refine their story-planning skills is to provide time for small-group critiques of the plan.

Refine Story Plans With Small-Group Critiques

I ask children to meet in groups of three to four students, no more. One child presents his plan. The others listen to make sure the problem is believable and is one that can be solved by the main character. Then they critique the episodes. Here are some questions to guide them:

- Would or could these things happen in this sequence? Do they seem likely? Do they suggest a struggle?
- Has the author planned for both external action and the internal reactions? Do things get worse before they get better?
- Finally, does the resolution satisfy the listener? Does the resolution follow logically from the episodes? Does the ending sound believable? Is it too neat and tidy, or does it sound like something that could happen to one of us?

Before looking for weaknesses in a story plan, you need to set a positive tone by stating all the good things the writer did in his plan. Critique means to critically look at both the strengths and the weaknesses. Possible comments from you, but preferably from students, could be:

- Your character is actively involved in all your episodes.
- Your setting adds urgency and suspense to your story.
- Your ending sounds believable.
- Your problem sounds typical for a twelve-year-old girl.
- Your story sounds logical and tightly focused on one main event.

Remind students to be thoughtful with their comments. The goal of a critique is to point out the strengths of the plan and then to mention one to three of the most critical weaknesses so the author can make adjustments to strengthen the story.

Fifth graders Lincoln Slentz and Eric Beckman work through episodes together to come up with a believable resolution. ▶

It is amazing to see all the inconsistencies that are caught when plans are critiqued. Some of the comments I've overheard in the years past are:

- "Your ending comes out of nowhere. Go back and let the ending follow naturally from what you've used in the episodes."
- "If you shorten the time that passes from the first episode to the last, the story's tension will be greater."
- "Your episodes need more struggle. Right now your character isn't really trying to solve the problem. He's just complaining about it."
- "First you told us that your character was in a cave; now, all of a sudden, he's in the woods. How did that happen?"

This planning can take anywhere from one to five days, depending on the amount of time you have each day. One way to support the students during this part of the process is to critique a few nearly completed plans together on the overhead projector. It's amazing how much your students will learn and remember about etiquette and plans that work.

Ready to Write

When the plans are completed, it's time to "write like the wind!" Now, instead of spending days and days organizing internally, writing and erasing, fretting and forgetting, students can refer to their plans and use rich language to make their stories sing.

Writing First Drafts

Before the students actually begin to write, I ask them to take a few moments to reread their plans. I want the children to think carefully about each episode. I prompt their thinking with questions like these:

Seventh grader Laura Gorman writes a first draft using her plan to guide her.

⊕ Do you have at least three solid events in your episodes?

⊕ Does the tension or conflict increase with each event?

⊕ Have you given yourself notes on internal as well as external conflict?

⊕ Are your events believable?

⊕ Does your character use any of his/her strengths to battle the problem?

⊕ Where does your story begin?

⊕ Do you want your story to begin with a pleasant or unpleasant event?

⊕ Will your character react quickly or thoughtfully?

Model Lesson: Last-Minute Revisions

I provide time for last-minute revisions. This additional thinking about their plans will help them later, when they critique their peers' plans. To increase their understanding of this part of the process, I model by placing one of my plans on the overhead and then raising questions about it:

EPISODES: 1. (external) After class, Dunk's teacher reminds him about the importance of the test.

   (internal) Dunk is worried—looks at what he needs to review, but doesn't want to miss out on basketball—it's his favorite.

2. (external) After school, Dunk's buddies ask him to join them for a basketball party and to shoot hoops.

   (internal) When he explains, his teammates tease him (somewhat angrily)—he feels left out like he let the team down, since he let his math go.

3. (external) Dunk asks the teacher for help—answer is no, too busy.

   (internal) He is overwhelmed—then remembers basketball advice he gives others when they're having a bad practice or game.

Questions I might ask myself are:

🌸 Where does Dunk's teacher speak with him? In the hall? In the room? Where his friends overhear? Is the teacher encouraging or does she sound disappointed in him?

🌸 How does Dunk show he is worried? What does his body do? What does he say to himself? What are his thoughts?

🌸 What are Dunk's buddies doing when he meets them? What do they say to him after he explains his predicament? What do they do that makes him feel left out?

🌸 Where does Dunk find his teacher? What does Dunk say? How does the teacher react?

🌸 What reminds Dunk of the advice he's given others in the past? What makes him think this advice will help him? How do his actions change after he remembers these words?

After posing these questions aloud, I might talk about where to start this story.

Brainstorming Beginnings

I'll brainstorm some possible beginnings, telling students that I want to get to the problem as soon as possible. I look at the first event on my story plan to find my promised starting point. Then I draft some possible beginnings:

🌸 <u>Brrrrrrring</u> sounded the bell ending math class. Finally, Dunk thought. Now I can meet up with the guys and see what's happening tonight. Just as he stepped out into the hall he heard his name being called by the math teacher, Mr. Burns. "Did you want me, sir?" Dunk asked as he stuck his head back into the classroom.

🌸 Dunk took his graded quiz back from his math teacher, Mr. Burns. Near the large D at the top, his teacher had added a note: [Please stay after class a few moments and speak with me today.] Dunk's stomach rolled. He knew his grades had been slipping in math. What did Mr. Burns want? Maybe he wanted to offer him tutoring?

🌸 "Dunk, could you please remain after class for a few moments?" asked Mr. Burns, his math teacher.

"Uh, sure, sir," Dunk answered.

After the classroom emptied, Dunk approached Mr. Burns' desk. "Does this have something to do with my low grades, Mr. Burns?" he asked.

"As a matter of fact, it does, Dunk," said Mr. Burns, looking serious.

LITERATURE LOOK

To give your students more models for effective beginnings, read aloud the opening lines of good literature. Try the first paragraph or two from:

🌸 *Backwater* by Joan Bauer

🌸 *If You Should Hear a Honey Guide* by April Pulley Sayre

🌸 *The Birthday Room* by Kevin Henkes

🌸 *Charlotte's Web* by E. B. White

🌸 *Baby* by Patricia MacLachlan

🌸 *Pink and Say* by Patricia Polacco

🌸 *Owl Moon* by Jane Yolen

I engage the students by asking them, Which opening sounds most natural? I then ask them which beginning pulled them into the story more quickly. While having the students look at their own plans, I guide them to their first event and suggest they start their story where that action begins.

Write!

Now it's time to "write like the wind." Encourage your students to get their stories down, without stopping or rereading. They can expand, delete, change, and revise in the next few days during critique sessions. Their only job now is to write their stories.

Here are some tips to make writing time productive:

Create a Quiet Environment. I have one major rule when it's writing time—no talking, whispering, or moving about. Most writers cannot work with distractions. As one of my fifth-grade students said one morning:

> *"It takes time to write. You need to go deep inside your well and it takes a while to do that. At first you notice what's going on around you, but eventually you begin to concentrate, and then you only see and hear the words in your head. I can't write when there's lots of activity going on around me. It keeps me from finding that place deep inside where I can think."*

Leave Room For Revision. I suggest that students leave three or four spaces between each line of the story. This helps during revision; they will have room to add details later on.

Encourage Students to Work Without Input. Some students will want you to help them write their rough drafts. Politely encourage those children to use their plans to write their own stories. Let them know there is no right or wrong way. Tell them to envision motion pictures of their stories in their heads and then ask them to write what they see.

Students write like the wind using their story plans as a guide.

Creating Story Titles

Within one to two class periods, most everyone will have their first draft completed. This is the first time I really encourage students to give some thought to their stories' titles. Even at this stage, I call them "working titles," so students see they can still easily change. To find the best title for a story, I ask students to look at a few different things in their writing. First, we consider the *main character's name*. Do we want to include it in the title? The next thing we concentrate on is the *problem*. Are there any key words used in referring to the problem that can be developed into an interesting title? The third thing we examine is the *turning point* of the story. Are there any specific words spoken here that can serve as a title? Does the character's insight, strength, courage, or inventiveness have its source here? After reviewing these specifics, students are usually able to come up with working titles.

I always tell students that a title is a lure. Just as the purpose of a fishing lure is to attract a fish to the bait, a title needs to attract a reader to the story. I ask them what criteria they use when choosing a book from the shelves of the library. What kinds of titles encourage them to begin reading a book? What kinds discourage them? I'm always impressed by the thought and effort they put into their titles. The best test of all, of course, is asking their peers what they think of their working titles.

First, Do Mini-Critiques: Beginnings

Before holding lengthy critique sessions, I like to look as a class at story openings in isolation. This study of openings gives everyone a break from writing and an opportunity for immediate feedback.

I ask permission to put a few students' opening sentences on the overhead. I remind students that the first two or three sentences have to hook the reader, and that most effective leads include the name of the main character, the setting, and a hint of the problem. This story beginning is taken from a piece of historical fiction entitled *Father and Spy* written by Eric Beckman, a fifth grader:

> *"Who's telling our secrets?" General Burgoyne screamed angrily. "When I find him, I'll have his hide."*
>
> *Samuel shuddered at these words. He knew he was that spy and that he'd have to be more careful taking the information back to Sam Adams or he would be caught.*

First, ask for comments that elicit the strengths, such as: Does the beginning pull the reader into the story? Can you identify the main character, setting, and the hint of the problem? Do you want to read more?

Students can even take overhead markers and show where the character, setting, and problem are represented in the first few sentences. Afterward,

without your suggestion, several students may decide to rewrite their openings.

Another quick way to conduct these mini-critiques is to have students volunteer to read their opening sentences. After reading his opening aloud, each volunteer can call on other students and ask them to identify the character, setting, and hint of the problem. If the audience cannot do this, then the writer knows he needs to rewrite that opening.

Let Students Take the Lead

I t is our natural inclination to be the main spokespersons during critiques. Please fight that urge. We need to be facilitators who ask the right questions and provide opportunities for the students to critique one another. We want to nurture in the children a keen awareness of others' writing and how to comment on that writing. If we are always the ones to validate or criticize, the students will never truly get involved. Instead, they will wait to see what we say. Ironically, after teachers take a backseat role during the critiques, the students stop expecting or soliciting the teacher's input and look exclusively to their peers. (Though this may be disconcerting at first, you'll quickly celebrate the students' independence and commitment.)

Some deftly written story endings can be found in:

⚙ *The Cay*
by Theodore Taylor

⚙ *Charlotte's Web*
by E. B. White

⚙ *Fly Away Home*
by Eve Bunting

⚙ *Jip: His Story*
by Katherine Paterson

⚙ *Missing May*
by Cynthia Rylant

Refining Endings

Endings can be just as much work as beginnings. As published authors will tell you, it's difficult to write one without revising the other. Many authors go back and rewrite beginnings once they know how the story actually ends.

When your students are writing endings, don't let them overstate. Young authors often want to finish a story by tacking on a moral—something like: "And from that day forward, Dunk never got behind in his math work again. The lesson we can learn from Dunk is, procrastination has no rewards." Since children don't like reading these endings, it seems funny that they try to create them. They probably write them because they think they make their stories sound complete.

Look at some effective story endings in books you have read together over the year. Point out how these books end with interesting and subtle resolutions rather than preachy and overemphasized lessons.

The Author's Voice

One of the great benefits of having students get their stories down quickly is that their writing voices have a much greater chance of emerging. "Voice" is one of the most difficult writing elements to explain, but one of the easiest to identify. It's the honesty, the purity of the author's diction. A writer usually "nails" this element when he becomes impassioned about the work at hand. In *What a Writer Needs* (Heinemann, 1993), Ralph Fletcher explains voice this way:

> *When I talk about voice, I mean written words that carry with them the sense that someone has actually written them. Not a committee, not a computer: a single human being. Writing with voice has the same quirky cadence that makes human speech so impossible to resist listening to… Developing voice in one's writing requires awareness and diligence; it probably also requires a patient, supportive mentor or writing teacher.*

Ironically, often the more "schooled" a student becomes, the tougher it is for him to find his voice. The younger the writer, the more naturally voice seeps into the writing. As children grow older, they perceive that there is one *right* way to write—one voice that must always be used, and the playfulness, lyrical flow, and wonder of their earlier writing seem to fall away.

What can we do to help students find their voices again? In her book *If You Want to Write* (Graywolf Press, 1987), Brenda Ueland reflects on how her students eventually broke away from trite and dull voices to write in a touching and true fashion:

> *What made them do this? I think I know. I think I helped them to do it. And I did not do it by criticism, i.e., by pointing out all the mediocrities in their efforts (and so making them contract and try nervously to avoid all sorts of faults). I helped them by trying to make them feel freer and bolder. Let her go! Be careless, reckless! Be a lion, be a pirate! Write any old way.*

Taking Ms. Ueland's advice, I give my students the charge: "Write free. Be bold. Say it your way." And I celebrate those times when I hear their true voices ring out.

Build Awareness of Voice Through Excellent Literature

An excellent way to help students become more aware of voice is to read and reread passages in books that exemplify a unique voice. The author Byrd Baylor captivates readers with her lyrical prose. Her passion for the natural world sings through all her books. She often weaves first, second, and third person points-of-view into her writing so that the reader is totally immersed in the subject and flow of language. You don't even realize what she's done until you stop and read like a writer. You might share her *If You Are a Hunter of Fossils* with your students and have them comment on the voice they hear. Let them describe how it sounds to them. How does it make them feel? about fossils? about the world? about the author? about themselves?

Each of Gary Paulsen's books has a distinct voice, but there is one passage that my students think has an extremely powerful voice. It's near the end of *The Rifle*—the last two paragraphs of the chapter entitled "The Joining." Students have asked me to read those lines over and over. The language is immediate, final, threatening, and remorseful, all at the same time.

For a playful voice, a voice that makes you giggle before you are aware you're doing so, read *The Scrambled States of America* by Laurie Keller. The language is quick, natural, and downright giddy at times.

Cynthia Rylant uses a sober, reflective voice in *Missing May*. A reader is charmed by the story, it's true, but somehow the voice engages readers on another level. Students seem to be lulled into self-reflection and a quiet reverie as they read. Later, when they discuss this book with one another, there is a reverence for the language and the story.

Who Came Down That Road by George Ella Lyon instills a sense of wonder. The voice is one of sincere curiosity. The reader joins with the child in this picture book and wants to know more about this road and the history surrounding it.

Students can identify voice once they are introduced to the power of it through good literature. That's why it's so important we select the best stories to share with them. The stronger the voices are in the books they read, the more likely our students will find their own.

I always point out strong voice in students' work. Sometimes a student doesn't fully know when she's "got it" until you tell her so!

This seventh-grade student used a distinct voice in her story *Suzie's Baby Sister*, which she wrote for children in grades K–2. Here is a portion of it:

"Suzie's Baby Sister"

by Laura Garman

Suzie hated babies.
Suzie hated diapers.
Suzie hated bottles.
Suzie hated cribs.
Suzie hated pacifiers.
Suzie hated babies.

"Great news, Suzie," said Suzie's mom. "You're gonna have a new baby sister!" Suzie was shocked. Suzie was stunned. Suzie was mad!
"No babies!" she said.
"Come on, Suzie, you love babies!" coaxed Suzie's mom.
"No," argued Suzie. "I hate babies!"
"I'll let you pick out her name. Any name you want. You can help me pick out her new furniture. Won't that be fun?" asked Suzie's mom.
"No. NO BABIES!" shouted Suzie.
"Why no babies?' asked her mom.
"Babies stink. Babies smell. Babies are bad. I HATE BABIES!" Suzie screamed.
"You were a baby once," her mom said.
"I was?" asked Suzie.
"Yes, you were. You were stinky, smelly, and bad, once in a while," said her mother.
"I was not! I'm not stinky, smelly, or bad!" Suzie argued.
"You're not now, but you used to be. See how you are now? Wouldn't you like to have a baby sister? I'll still let you pick out her name," said her mom.
"I don't care!" screamed Suzie.

What voice! This seventh grader beautifully matched the voice to the age of the character. Notice her sentence length and choice of vocabulary; it's short and snappy. How did this writer succeed? She knew and loved her subject matter. While we cannot count on every student finding his voice in every piece—far from it—we *can* keep nudging our students to write about things that matter to them. To find voice, a writer has to feel passion, and has to be writing from personal experience.

A Few Words About Point of View

When teaching point of view, I keep a few things in mind. First of all, most children write in the third person. It's "safe" and it's the point of view they encounter the most in their reading. This is fine, and we need not change it. For beginning story writers, it works best if they use the third person consistently throughout their stories. There are some gifted writers who can flip-flop between points of view, but most students find that difficult, not to mention confusing.

Point of view is difficult to teach, and tough to learn. Whether students write in the third person or the first person, the main goal is to have their stories unfold through their main characters. The reader will want to stay focused on the events from that character's viewpoint. Therefore, the writer will have to make sure to flesh that person out so that we understand his/her feelings, actions, and personal struggle and gain.

Celebrate and Reflect

With their first drafts written, students are ready to celebrate. This is a wonderful time to refer back to the writing process circle you've had on display. Look at all the stages you've visited and revisited. Discuss which parts of the process were most challenging and helpful. Have students read aloud passages from their first drafts where they think their writer's voice sings. Share phrases that are specific and add detail to their stories. Ask them if they are pleased with their first drafts. Tell them that now it's time to look carefully at what they've written well and what they would like to improve. It's time to critique and revise for deeper meaning and clarity.

CHAPTER 8

Revising for Meaningful Change

R evision can be a daunting process, especially if the student's first experience involves a lengthy story of ten pages or so. Since I want students to be successful at revision, understand its role in the process, and enjoy it, I offer revision lessons and strategies that are limited in focus. In this chapter, I share them with you. Let's first look at one I give my students early in the year, called "Rewrites."

Fifth graders Marie McKinnon and Kimberly Troyer exchange first drafts and offer suggestions.

Revision Strategy: Rewrites

A "rewrite" is a short, weak passage I've drafted. I place it on the overhead projector, and then invite students to point out strengths and weaknesses. After students have established two or three main areas of concern and brainstormed ways to improve these, they independently rewrite the passage so it will convey its meaning more effectively.

While the rewrite pieces always emphasize the content of the writing, I slant them for different purposes. For example, sometimes the piece lacks organization. "No plan!" the students will exclaim right away. Some rewrites have no focus or use weak vocabulary. Sometimes the flow from sentence to sentence is almost nonexistent. I never overload a rewrite. For instance, I don't mix editing concerns with issues of style and content. All my rewrites have correct grammar, punctuation, and spelling. I don't want students getting sidetracked on grammar when their concentration needs to be on content.

Sample Rewrite Session

I try to match subject matter with age and interest level. The following rewrite passage could be used successfully with most students in grades four and above, because they can easily relate to this experience:

The boy lunged at the dog. His hands grabbed the dog and held on tight. The dog twisted and turned. He tried to get away. The boy had the hose. He put it over the dog's head and body. The dog got wet. So did the boy.

At first we list the strengths of this passage. For the first few rewrites, you will need to prompt the students with specific questions. For example:

* Is this piece focused on one topic?
* Do you know the main character?
* Can you easily keep track of what's happening?
* Is the writing clear?
* Is there use of strong, specific vocabulary?
* Does one thought flow easily into the next?
* Does this piece hold your attention or make you want to read more?

Always guide students toward the matters of craft you want them to refine with questions regarding focus, meaning, clarity, vocabulary, fluency, voice, and logical sequence. In the past, students have noted these strengths when discussing this rewrite:

Vocabulary: lunged, twisted and turned

Focus: It stays with one event.

Action: There is something definitely happening.

The following weaknesses have also been pointed out. NOTE: I never let students list more than three weaknesses. Otherwise they get lost trying to address too much in the rewrite:

Sequence: needs to be clearer

Who's who?: For specific vocabulary and clarity, we need a name for the boy, at least, and maybe a name for the dog; use fewer pronouns (he) and more specific references.

Details: needs details to add spark and interest

Fourth graders and I collaboratively rewrite a short passage on the overhead. They offer suggestions of specific verbs to make the writing more vivid. ▶

Our next step is to brainstorm specific ways to improve this writing. I list these ways on the overhead right beneath the rewrite passage so that students can use them as a reference. Students have offered these suggestions:

◉ Make a short plan to improve the order of the story. Plan:

Who:	boy
Where:	backyard
When:	Saturday afternoon
What:	Boy needs to wash his Great Dane, Otto.
Details:	Boy has to trick dog.
	Dog tries to get away.
	Boy gets dog under the hose.
	Boy gets wet.

⚙ Name the boy and the dog (the students usually want to do this as a class):

Boy: Fletcher

Dog: Otto

Details: Where and when is this happening?

What are the difficulties?

What other tools does the boy use?

How did the boy get wet?

With these good ideas in place, students take 15 to 25 minutes to rewrite this passage, each using his own vocabulary, voice, and personal experiences. I write, too. A finished version may look like this:

It was the third Saturday of the month—Otto's bath day. Ten-year-old Fletcher knew a treat would help coax his Great Dane toward the hose. So, with salami in hand, Fletcher led Otto into the backyard near the outdoor spigot. He slowly reached down, turned on the water and picked up the hose. Otto sprang toward the house. Fletcher lunged forward and grabbed the dog around his collar with one hand. Otto twisted and turned, back and forth. Fletcher held tight, like a cowboy on a bucking bronco. With his free hand, he held the hose over Otto's head and sprayed. Otto froze, water dripping off his ears and down his sides. Quickly, Fletcher squeezed a dab of dog shampoo across his pet's back. He scratched and scrubbed, up and down, over and under, until Otto was a sudsy statue. With his last bit of strength, Fletcher rinsed Otto from head to tail and fell back into the grass. For his thank you, Otto shook and shook and shook, leaving Fletcher needing a shampoo, too.

I help a student brainstorm word choices during revision. A dictionary or a thesaurus is often a good tool for this. ▷

Afterward, in groups of three or four, everyone reads their rewrites out loud. Students love this sharing as much as the quick-write readings. Even though everyone started with the same general information, none of the pieces sound anything alike. Sometimes I ask if anyone has heard a rewrite that he thinks should be shared with the whole group. Usually, a few students then read their rewrites aloud to the entire class.

Why is this successful? Everyone receives practice in identifying strengths and weaknesses in writing. The rewrite is short enough to be reworked rather quickly, in 15–25 minutes. Students see how revision clarifies meaning and adds focus and spark to writing. It teaches children to look at their own stories in chunks and revise section by section to improve them. Plus, students enjoy it. We want positive attitudes toward revision, and this is one place to start.

Revision Strategy: Turn "Tells" Into "Shows"

Writing teachers often caution their students, "Show, don't tell." It's good advice. When we *show*, we keep the reader engaged in the story with active language. By using similes, metaphors, and sensory words that evoke sounds, smells, tastes, and visual images, we quickly engage our reader, drawing him right into the action of the story. When we *tell* a story, we keep our reader at a distance, eliminating the details and description that make the story come alive.

One of my favorite activities to conduct with student writers is "Turn Tells Into Shows." I begin by placing examples of active writing on the overhead projector, like the following excerpt from *Riding Freedom* by Pam Munoz Ryan:

> *The next morning, Charlotte woke to the sounds of a busy stable. Stock tenders called to one another. Bridles and traces jangled. The stable master barked out orders. Charlotte peered over the edge of the loft and barely moved. She couldn't just climb down and appear. They might throw her out. She listened to the comings-and-goings for some hours until things settled down. Maybe it was lunchtime.*
>
> *When no one was moving about and all she could hear was the blow and whinnies of the horses, she pushed up the loft window. It opened onto a low roof. She quietly climbed out, shinnied down a wooden support beam, and landed behind the main barn.*

I read aloud the passage and invite students to come to the overhead projector and underline in colored marker the words and phrases they feel make this writing come alive, the parts that are *show* rather than *tell*. Their usual choices are:

- Stock tenders called to one another.
- Bridles and traces jangled.
- The stable master barked out orders.
- Charlotte peered over the edge of the loft
- all she could hear was the blow and whinnies of the horses
- shinnied down a wooden support beam

As they underline, students talk about how descriptive the writing is and even use the words *show* and *tell*. They single out words and phrases they really like, noting, for example, how "shinnied down the wooden support beam" is much more of a *show* and consequently much more interesting than "went down the support beam." The contrast is helpful. I've seen them apply this understanding to their critique sessions and revision time. Students begin to distinguish a "show" from a "tell" quickly and exhibit their awareness in their own stories and comments.

I repeat this exercise with passages from:

- *Mississippi Bridge* by Mildred D. Taylor
- *Blackwater* by Eve Bunting
- *Wait Till Helen Comes* by Mary Downing Hahn

After students are confident with this procedure, I give them rewrites and ask them to identify the tells and turn them into shows. I begin with a sentence: *She sat on the bed and cried.* Students' rewrites might look like these:

```
Marie crouched on the bed and sobbed.


The mother sat on the end of her daughter's bed,
afghan in hand, and wept silently for the loneliness
                 she felt in her heart.


Frustrated with her own jealousy, Jillian threw
   herself onto the bed and cried until her eyes
                were swollen and red.
```

Similarly, to help students to show characters' feelings, we discuss how boring it is to read, "He was happy," or "She was angry." I write this passage, and ask them to rewrite it so that Kyle's emotions are conveyed through action and details:

Kyle was frightened. He had never been this scared.

Students' rewrites might look like these:

> Kyle felt the blood drain from his face and neck.
> He tried to push his feet forward, but fear cemented
> them to the floor.
>
> Kyle heard the sirens, like the shrill call of witches,
> right outside his window. The wild flames licked
> his walls with ruby tongues and slid closer
> to his shaking body.

After the students have practiced turning tells into shows, I place a passage of four or five sentences on the overhead projector. We read it, discuss the more mundane parts, and brainstorm ways in which language could strengthen the meaning. Then everyone, including me, rewrites the passage. We share with partners and then read a few out loud to the whole group. The writer receives only positive feedback for what he did right.

Critiques

Many educators use the term *conference* to refer to the time when students and teachers meet individually to read and discuss stories in the production stage. I have to admit that earlier in my career, I did try to get to as many students as possible and conference with them about their writing. Maybe it was due to my poor conferencing skills, but I found that students didn't seem to take this time seriously. Or, should I say, I didn't see concrete changes taking place in their work as a direct result of these conferences. Plus, I got frustrated that I could only meet with a few students each day, and that left many to proceed unattended.

Meanwhile, as I continued with my own writing, I would gather with colleagues for a group *critique*, during which we would examine the strengths and weaknesses of our first drafts. I brought the structure of these critique sessions back to my classroom, and discovered it works well.

1 Begin with general, positive comments about the strength of the piece as a whole. Ask questions of the writer, such as: Why did you write this piece? Who is your intended audience?

2 Discuss story elements. Explore such questions as: Is the character believable? Is the problem compelling? Do the events build tension within the story? Is there a reasonable resolution?

3 If, and only if, all of the above is on track does the critique move to discuss point of view, word choice, grammar, and other fine points.

▲ *Seventh graders peer-critique one another's stories.*

Modeling Critiques

After students complete their first drafts, a critique is the next step. I always ask the writer whose work is being critiqued to bring a pencil to the session so that he can add revisions as we go along. We put his story on the overhead, and I use a marker to note revisions on the overhead. With all eyes following the text, the writer reads the story out loud. After the first read, anyone can offer initial positive comments. this is an excellent time to comment on the whole story. Model the types of questions you want students to ask. Ask the writer about purpose and audience. Why did he choose this topic? This character? Find out if there is a personal investment in some aspect of the story.

The next step is to make specific positive comments about elements of the story. Even the weakest story has something going for it right from the beginning:

⚙ Your title is strong. It gives a hint of the story without giving away the ending.

⚙ Your character was so spunky. She added a lot of spark to the story.

⚙ Your topic—divorce—is difficult, but you just examined one tiny part of that in your story.

⚙ Clever ending—I didn't even think it would end that way.

Before we begin mentioning weaknesses, the writer often makes a specific request for feedback on a particular problem he encountered. This might be something that he struggled with while writing the story. It might be a weak spot in the plan. It could be that he wants suggestions to improve the title. We always give the author an opportunity to ask something of the group. Encourage the writer to begin with a general question that elicits the strengths of his writing first:

1   **What did I do well?**

2   **Is the story focused?**

3   **Do you understand the story?**

4   **Does it hold your interest?**

5   **Any suggestions for a different title?**

6   **What needs improvement?**

Then the writer can ask more specific ones:

✿ I had trouble with the ending. Does it seem like it's a good ending for the story, or does it seem tacked on?

✿ Do you care about my character? Do you think she is likable?

✿ Is there a way I could add more tension to my episodes?

✿ My titles seem a little blah. Any suggestions for a different one?

Then the author reads the story out loud again. This time everyone is really examining the strengths and weaknesses, because they are already somewhat familiar with the story. After the second reading, the author needs to manage his own critique group. The student would ask the class for specific suggestions to improve character, problem, events, or resolution. Most writers can revise two to four aspects of their story at a time. It is a good idea to keep the suggestions limited to five minutes.

At the beginning of the year it is helpful if the elements of strong story writing are posted in the room to guide discussion. This can be a simple list that reads: *Focus, Meaning, Fluency, Voice, Character, Setting, Problem, Conflict, Resolution, Character Growth.*

Using Rubrics in Class Critiques

So, to recap: Every critique begins with positive comments. Then, we address the questions the author posed to us. Finally, using a rubric as a guide, students critique the story on issues of craft. For instance, if the rubric uses the criteria listed below, these form the starting point for the critique. We pay the most attention to the first three criteria; the last—varied sentence structure—is addressed later during the editing process.

	EXCELLENT	GOOD	NEEDS WORK
Believable Character	Character speaks and acts like a child of that age.	Most of character's speech and action are appropriate for a child that age.	Character seems artificial, has few similarities to a real child.
Episodes Develop Conflict	Three or more episodes build conflict in a realistic way.	At least two episodes add to story's conflict.	Conflict is difficult to recognize; character doesn't struggle.
Title Attracts Reader	Title lures reader into story without giving away ending.	interesting title, carries meaning attached to the story	nothing interesting about the title
Varied Sentence Structure	At least four different sentence structures are used.	Three different sentence structures are used.	One or two different sentence structures are used.

Model Good Critique Questions

In the beginning, it's helpful to guide student authors to ask the kinds of questions that will spark constructive ideas for their stories. For example, I might ask:

- Could you imagine knowing a child like this one?
- What details in the story made this character seem real?
- Was there any behavior or language that seemed unnatural to you?

I've never seen students accept anything less than a believable character. Remember, they know kid characters best, how they act and what they say. Next, I might ask:

- Can you identify the basic action of each episode?
- Did the tension get a little tighter in the second episode?
- Was the tension even stronger by the third episode?
- Which details seemed natural to you? Were there any that seemed contrived?
- Did you feel a sense of urgency as the story continued?
- Did the author show us how the character felt as events happened?
- Can you point out the exact places where feelings are shown, not told?

For the title, I might ask:

- Did the title grab you a little before the story was read?
- Do you think the title goes with this story?
- Can you think of any way to improve upon this title?

As the facilitator, try to curb an excess of negative comments. When setting the ground rules for critiques, I let students know that since we are here to suggest ideas for improvement, we only mention a concern once. If several children notice the same weakness in a story, they may all confirm what another student mentions but not dwell on the same issue over and over.

Have the Author Write Down Responses

While the students offer suggestions, the author writes notes in the margins and spaces between lines. These need to be written clearly, so that when the author returns to his desk to work on revisions, he can read what was said. Again, as the facilitator, you may have to remind students to wait in between suggestions until the author has finished recording the previous comment. Once students start discussing a piece, they want to go very quickly from point to point.

I've also used another strategy with great success. Sometimes the audience writes their suggestions for revisions on scraps of paper for the writer to review later. We try to be as specific as possible: "*On page 2, your tension dropped off when the main character didn't react to the second snake. It's as if he isn't afraid anymore. You might rework that part.*" When the author receives written comments, he can take more time to decide which criticisms warrant change and which ones he wants to ignore.

End with a Positive Statement

Another ground rule we have is that each class critique must end with a positive statement. We want the author to know we really see what he is doing well, and that we are supporting him in his efforts to improve his story. The ending comment might be something like:

- ⚙ I heard a strong voice coming through your writing—smooth and calm.
- ⚙ This story grabs you from the first sentence.
- ⚙ Your story has a strong character and a good problem.
- ⚙ Your details showed the action well.

Small-Group Critiques

After practicing with the whole group on a few students' first drafts, it's time to have the students meet in small groups (three or four children) and critique one another. Those students who just received a class critique with the whole group need to join a small group and help their peers. It's good to have the ground rules and procedure posted in the room or on a sheet for students to use as a reference. (See page 141 for sample ground rules and procedures.)

Usually the same group of students will meet together until they each complete one story. In fact, some students like to have a second critique session after they have made their revisions. I prefer that this request come from the students. If I'm patient and wait, someone usually requests it, and then it snowballs. Other students would like to know if their revisions are working and what else they can now do to improve their stories. For future writing, new critique groups are formed. This gives everyone a chance to hear different classmates' stories throughout the year.

I make sure to circulate between groups, listening to one full critique each time. The biggest reminder I offer students is to limit comments to ones involving the criteria on the rubrics. I also urge them not to get carried away with criticism. If students overload their classmate with too much helpful advice, the writer may just give up and not revise at all.

The Writer Has Final Say

Everyone in our community of writers understands that not every piece of criticism will necessarily be used. Sometimes a word change is suggested yet the author stays with his original choice—or a different ending is posed. The writer may not be totally pleased with the present ending but knows she does not want to use the suggestion. Instead of arguing or becoming defensive, we try to accept all comments and write them down. Later, in private, we can evaluate and use the critical comments that best meet our needs.

Revision

After students have received input from their fellow writers, it's time to revise. As I stated earlier, I don't encourage students to revise everything all at once. I tell them to start with one chunk and see what can be done to improve it. I also ask them to weigh the comments from the critique group and then revise as best as they can. When the students complete some of their revisions, they like feedback. I let them call short, impromptu critique meetings to listen to the changes and provide comments. This is one of our goals—to have students become so involved in their stories that they'll want to revise, share, and revise further.

Targeting Students Who Need Support

During the final stages of revision, students work and share, work and share, until they feel their stories are complete. I've never known revision to last more than two class periods. Some students will have revised some chunks five times; some students will barely have revised once all the way through. I use to get extremely frustrated with this disparity. Then I began speaking to students about their stories. The children who had an emotional investment in their stories really wanted to continue revising. Those who wrote to please others, or to fill writing time, wanted revision over with as quickly as possible. I learned to target the latter group of students with more of my individual time. I found it was crucial to help them select more personal topics for story ideas.

 I help a fifth grader work through his revision, and together we consult a rubric for guidance.

Celebrating Each New Step

Teaching writing takes time and patience. Eventually, all children want to be a part of the writing community. Our goal is to help each writer grow. They all do it at different rates and at different times. Our job is to be there offering the most support we can and celebrating each new step.

With revision completed, students are ready to polish their stories through the editing process. It can be painless, almost enjoyable, when the children learn strategies to become independent editors.

Edit and Publish for an Audience

A student reads her published story to peers. It's important to give students a forum for sharing their finished work.

All students need to know why and how to edit. For years, many teachers did a complete edit of all student writing. Typically, the teacher would take the students' writing home, red-pencil in corrections, and return the papers to the authors. Many of us now know that this provided wonderful practice for the teacher but little understanding of the purpose and process of editing for the students.

In the Random House Webster's Dictionary (1996), the second definition for the word edit is "*to prepare for publication*." An edit involves correcting sentence construction, spelling, grammar, and punctuation. Afterward, the piece is ready for the public. Every teacher of student writers has his own philosophy about editing. Select the workable parts of the following editing plan to meet the needs of your students.

Making Meaning Clear

We need to tell students that the purpose of editing is to clarify meaning by using the conventions of our language correctly. If poor spelling, grammar, or punctuation constantly distracts readers, they will lose the meaning of the story. Learning how to edit will improve all of our writing.

I don't believe that every story that every child writes needs to be published in book form or to be put on public display. In fact, I believe that much of the writing we do in schools needs to be just practice. I know that many of my first efforts, and some of my current efforts, will never be published, but each of these pieces has helped me learn about writing and revision. Students need opportunities to grow as writers, too. Through practice they gain knowledge, insight, problem-solving skills, writing strategies, revision techniques—and hopefully, a love of writing. In my classroom, students enjoy writing and revising three to five stories a year, then selecting their favorite for publication.

Use Rubric Criteria as Guidelines

On any rubric you use for story writing, there ought to be at least one criterion for grammar. And there needs to be a mini-lesson from you on that particular point. For instance, a teacher can ask permission from a student and place a transparency on the overhead projector of a passage from her story. The class can then evaluate it in light of the standards for sentence structure listed in the rubric below:

	EXCELLENT	AVERAGE	NEEDS WORK
Varied Sentence Structure	use of varied sentence structure througout the story	two different sentence structures used	basic sentence repeated again and again

A Look at Sentence Variety

The following is the ending of a piece of historical fiction written by a fifth-grade student:

"A Time of Hope"
by Lindie Hohler

Marcus stumbled over to the tomb and sat in the warm sand. Mother, he thought, this is for you—for your love, your care, your hope. I know you're watching over me and I know you're probably proud. I have something to tell you that I've never said before. I love you and I miss you. Tears started flowing down his cheek, glistening in the evening sun. All he could do now was wait.

A low cry of agony came from the window above him. It was done. Cleopatra was gone. Marc Antony was gone. Caesar was gone. Would Egypt be gone without the guidance of Cleopatra? That is one answer only time would tell.

With this passage on the overhead projector, I ask a student to come up and underline one sentence construction and identify it. If the child selects the first sentence, he might say it has a compound predicate. If the child has less knowledge of the conventions of grammar, he might say the sentence says two things that Marcus does. If the next child underlines the second-to-last sentence, he may point out that it is a question. Already we have two different types of sentences in just one passage. Another student may contrast the four short sentences containing only subject and verb that begin with "It was done," with the lengthier sentences of the first part that include prepositional phrases. It is clear that this writer has used varied sentence structure in just one small part of her story.

When examining story passages for varied sentence structure, it is not important that students know all the correct grammatical terms. The important thing is that they notice sentence variety. When authors vary their writing with questions, short noun-verb sentences, and lengthier detailed sentences, their work takes on a rhythm and a voice that grabs the reader.

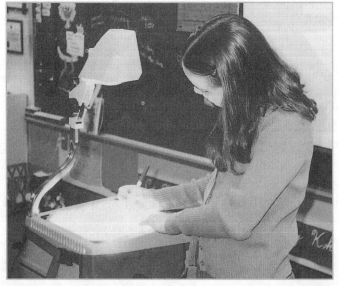

▲ *Lindie asks for a peer critique of her story from the class.*

I then put another sample on the overhead projector to point out more constructions. Students are asked to identify 3 or 4 different types of sentences in their stories. If they can't, I tell them that this is an opportunity to add more variety before the final draft is written. But the most important part of this mini-lesson is to learn *why* a writer uses these different constructions.

Referring to the *A Time of Hope* sample, I ask why the author used those four short sentences near the end. How did these change the tone of the piece? What was she trying to do? Why wouldn't long, flowing sentences have worked well there? Why did this author insert a question near the end? What did that do for the ending of the story? Writers don't change sentence structures on a whim. All choices about language are made to enhance the flow and meaning of a piece. Therefore, the most important question is: *How does the blend of these sentences help the author communicate meaning?*

Editing for Spelling

Every child is responsible for the criteria listed on the rubrics whether the story is made public or not. If the choice is made to publish a story, then the student needs to edit the entire story. Some spelling errors can be avoided during the planning stages. While I circulate among students, reading their story plans, I nudge writers to correct their spellings of the names of main characters, places, or objects that will be repeated in the story. Sometimes I underline the word so they know to look up the correct spelling. Other times, I pencil in the correct spellings at the top of their plans as a support for them as they continue. It's easier to help students identify spelling weaknesses now, during this planning stage, than later on, when twenty-seven first drafts are ready to be edited.

During that final spelling edit, I do not go from paper to paper, circling all misspelled words. Instead, I suggest students reread their stories and each circle five words with possible spelling errors. They are then asked to look them up in the dictionary.

I don't have a problem with student published work that has a misspelled word here or there as long as a real effort has been made to correct most of the spelling errors. Again, students are learners practicing their skills. A disclaimer can always be added to the final story when it is published. It can state that the author has edited the story with care, but a few errors may have slipped through.

Sixth graders Erica Wilson and Laura Gorman work together to correct punctuation and spelling.

Editing for Grammar and Punctuation

Grammar and punctuation are two more areas of concern. We learn to check for subject-verb agreement, pronoun-antecedent agreement, same-tense agreement, and correct use of commas, apostrophes, quotation marks, colons, and semicolons. Taught within the context of a story, these editing skills have more meaning. I also sit one-on-one with students who need extra support in these areas during their first and final drafts. I never fix things for them outright, but I do try to fi.̃d a few examples in their writing for us to correct together. Our goal is not to intervene until every story is an editing marvel but rather to equip students with strategies that will help them grow as editors of their own work.

Seventh graders read one another's work during the editing phase.

Evaluating With the Rubric

When revision and editing are complete, it's time to evaluate strengths and weaknesses. Students use their rubrics for this final assessment. As stated in Chapter 2, the author rereads his story and then works through the rubric one criterion at a time. I often lead the students through their evaluations the first and second times. That's all it takes before they understand the process. After each student has placed X's on the boxes reflecting his achievement, he exchanges his story with a peer. The peer reads the story twice, once to learn the story line and the second time to study story structure. The peer marks the rubric with a different colored pencil. If there is disagreement about the author's achievement, the two evaluators must discuss their opinions and document from the story until there is an agreement.

For lengthy stories, peer evaluation can take 30 to 45 minutes, especially if there is a difference of opinion, but afterward, the student can easily identify his strengths as a story writer within the evaluated piece. There is nothing nebulous about assessing with rubrics. Students can always support their opinions through direct references to story elements or audience response. However, as with all opinions, some subjectivity can enter into the decision. Rubrics are not completely foolproof, but they do provide students with a much more comprehensive understanding of their strengths and weaknesses as a writer than does a teacher's grade written across the top of the story.

Sometimes students try to give a friend all "Excellent" evaluations just to please him. It's our job to sit down with those students and help them make direct references to the story to substantiate their claims. To be honest, I have only had that happen a few times, and it was always at the beginning of the process. As students continue to learn more about the craft of story writing, they appreciate the workmanship that goes into each piece, and they will not compromise standards. If you are not pleased with student use of rubrics, it's a good idea to slow down and use simpler ones until they learn to evaluate more effectively.

As I stated in Chapter 2, the real power of rubrics is established when the students and teacher draw up the list of criteria together. When students make this initial investment, they tend to work harder to meet these standards, no matter where they are in the writing process. Students and teachers select criteria that are fundamental to a good story. The choices all reflect mini-lessons and demonstrations that have been a part of the learning environment.

The process is almost complete. There is always a choice about how stories will be shared. Please remember that to complete the cycle, a writer must share his story with an authentic audience. Then, and only then, is the real purpose of writing satisfied.

Classroom Publishing

Now our stories are ready to be published. There are several good references on the market that describe unique book and illustration design. Here are a few you may consider adding to your classroom library:

- *75 Creative Ways to Publish Students' Writing* by Cherlyn Sunflower
- *Books Don't Have to Be Flat! Innovative Ways to Publish Students' Writing in Every Curriculum Area* by Kathy Pike and Jean Mumper
- *Creative Bookbinding* by Pauline Johnson
- *Cover to Cover: Creative Techniques for Making Beautiful Books, Journals, and Albums* by Shereen Laplantz
- *Easy Bookmaking: Thematic Pop-Ups, Cards, and Shape Books* by Natalie Walsh
- *How a Book Is Published* by Bobbie Kalman
- *How to Make Super Pop-Ups* by Joan Irvine and Linda Hendry
- *Making Books That Fly, Fold, Wrap, Hide, Pop up, Twist & Turn* by Gwen Diehn
- *Write and Illustrate Your Own Book* by Chimeric Inc. Staff
- *How to Write, Illustrate, and Produce Your Own Book* by Donna Guthrie, Nancy Bentley, and Katy Keck Arnsteen

Every self-contained classroom needs access to a few of these books, assorted art supplies, and binding materials. Book production, if that is the chosen means for publication, does not need to be elaborate. In fact, I sometimes think this is one reason children get turned-off by story writing. It can take some students a month to complete 10–12 illustrations, plus a cover. Instead, allow students to select one to three scenes to illustrate thoroughly, adding meaning to their text with the use of art.

CHAPTER 10

Writing Stories Across the Curriculum

W riting stories can be one of the ways teachers identify what students understand in their studies. Several years ago one of my students wrote a story entitled *Where's My Leopard?* After reading his story, I knew what leopards ate, how they slept, their dangers, their strengths, and daily habits. This information didn't overwhelm me, because it was gently filtered into the main conflict. His story helped me understand

A student illustrates her story.

what a powerful tool stories can be across the curriculum. Let's look at a few examples that have worked well for my students.

Cumulative Stories

A cumulative story begins with one fundamental line, such as, "*This is the house that Jack built.*" Each new page adds another line to extend the meaning and build the story: "*This is the malt, that lay in the house that Jack built.*" "*This is the rat, that ate the malt, that lay in the house that Jack built.*"

I explain a cumulative story to children as one that accumulates lines, one on top of another, until the entire story is told. Cumulative stories are easy to read and enjoy. From the first time we hear *The House That Jack Built*, we recognize the rhythm and basic story structure. In preparing to write our own cumulative stories, the students and I read and reread *The Napping House* by Audrey Wood and *The House That Crack Built* by Clark Taylor. Of course, we first talk about the meaning and how the rhythm and rhyme never interfere with what the story is saying. I always tell students that their cumulative stories do not have to rhyme. We talk about forced rhyme and how it detracts from the meaning. To understand the structure of a cumulative story, we diagram one of these books in simple form.

Use a Diagram to Connect Scenes with Linking Verb

Making this simple-step diagram helps students see how the nouns, or scenes, are hooked to the previous scene with a verb. That's why the key noun is listed in the box and the connecting verb is listed on the bracket. Once they see that the verb links the two scenes and has an important meaning, it is easier for a student to plan a cumulative story that flows. For some students, though, all they need to do is sit with pencil and paper, and the entire story line comes at once.

A Diagram of the Development of the Cumulative story
The House That Crack Built

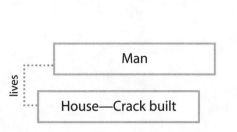
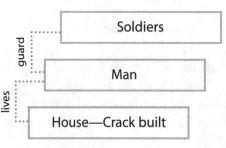
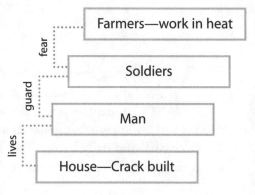

Make a Guiding Plan

If a student chooses to write a cumulative story to present a cycle in the real world, I encourage him to make some sort of a plan. This helps him decide what important information will go into the story. As with all plans, it can be changed as the writer develops his ideas and sees a need to add or delete information. Plans are always skeletal; they don't reflect the descriptive language or voice of the piece. They are simply road maps that lead to a well-organized story.

A fourth grader wrote this cumulative story after an independent study of skin cancer in her health/science class. It is easy to see what information made an impact on her during her research.

"A Painful Cancer"
by Jennifer Nagel, fourth grader

This is the sun, shining bright.

This is the woman, pretty and thin,
who loves the sun, shining bright.

This is the tan, dark and deep,
on the woman, pretty and thin,
who loves the sun, shining bright.

(Continued on next page)

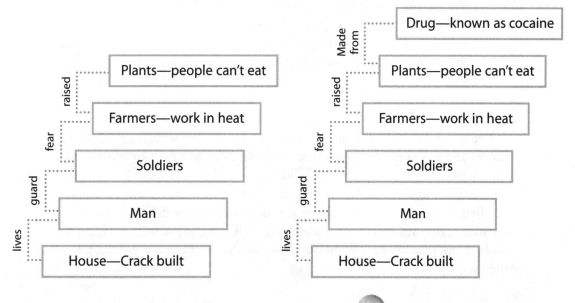

(Continued from page 117)

This is the sunburn that flakes off
from the tan, dark and deep,
on the woman, pretty and thin,
who loves the sun, shining bright.

This is a mole, enlarged and sore,
from many sunburns, that flake off
from the tans, dark and deep,
on the woman, pretty and thin,
who loves the sun, shining bright.

This is the doctor that found the tumor,
formed by the mole, enlarged and sore,
from many sunburns, that flake off
from the tan, dark and deep,
on the woman, pretty and thin,
who loves the sun, shining bright

This is skin cancer, caused by the sun,
diagnosed by the doctor as a tumor,
formed by the mole, enlarged and sore,
from many sunburns, that flake off,
from the tans, dark and deep,
on the woman, pretty and thin,
who loves the sun, shining bright.

This is the pain, felt by the family,
from her cancer, caused by the sun,
diagnosed by the doctor as a tumor,
formed by the mole, enlarged and sore,
from many sunburns, that flake off,
from the tan, dark and deep,
on the woman, pretty and thin,
who loves the sun, shining bright.

I've learned from experience that we need to expose students to different genres and forms of writing so that they select the best ones to express themselves. Of course, years ago I didn't realize this, and I would nurse the whole class through one form at a time. And, predictably, some students excelled at certain kinds of writing and others had great difficulty. Now, after observing students more carefully, I realize my job is to provide literary tools. They themselves will choose the tools that best convey the meaning they want to share.

Round Stories

"Round story" is a term I give to a story that comes full circle. It is typically written about a natural cycle and uses one simple word as a link between terms. At first I hesitated to include this form here because of its simplicity, but then I remembered the fun students had with it. Its basic structure can be just the support some children need to be successful story writers. Since the form is patterned, all thought and problem-solving efforts can be focused on selecting the most appropriate and meaningful terms.

It can also be used as a tool to evaluate student comprehension of specific material. Again, this type of story works better with a cycle, whether in science, social studies, health, or math. If children want to write a story using this form, I read *Night Becomes Day* by Richard McGuire. We discuss how this author presents a very broad cycle. It works in his book, but most students are more successful if they maintain a tighter focus.

List the Different Stages

For a brief plan, a student needs to decide on the subject matter and then quickly list words that represent the different stages of the cycle in the order they occur. Of course, for the story to be "round" it must come around full circle.

For instance, last year I worked with a class of fourth graders. Their teacher wanted us to write about popcorn to coordinate with a food study. We first discussed the different stages of popcorn from planting to eating. Then we generated a list:

field	green	silk	snack
fertile	grow	pollination	compost
cultivated	vibrant	kernels	earth
rows	ripe	harvest	field
planted	tassel	heat	fertile
seeds	flower	steam	
seedlings	pollen	POP!	
stalks	airborne	food	

Originally our list contained words like *pick, factory, package,* and *consumer.* After we talked about it, we decided on a tighter focus and having just one person grow and eat the popcorn. Our first list did not have anything about pollination. A student asked where her knowledge of pollen fit into this story and we added that chunk. The children read and reread their list before agreeing it was time to proceed. Next, we selected our connective word. In a round story, the same word is repeated throughout the text to connect the images. For some stories, *becomes* works well. For other round stories, students need a word that joins their terms in a different way.

Finding the Best Connective Verb

For the water cycle a child might use the verb *makes*. Sun makes heat, heat makes evaporation, evaporation makes water vapor, water vapor makes clouds, and so on. If a student wants to write a round story about bicycle movement, the connective term can be *turn*. Feet turn pedals, pedals turn the front sprocket, the front sprocket turns the chain, the chain turns the back sprocket, the back sprocket turns the back wheel, the back wheel turns the front wheel, and so it goes. The trick is to find the verb that best describes the action connecting cause to effect throughout the story.

At right is our final popcorn story, in which we used the verb *become*.

This story reflects a thorough understanding of how popcorn comes from a field and develops through pollination. Round stories give children a lighthearted way to respond to the curriculum.

"Popcorn Becomes Food"

Field becomes fertile.
Fertile becomes cultivated.
Cultivated becomes rows.
Rows become planted.
Planted becomes seeds.
Seeds become seedlings.
Seedlings become stalks.
Stalks become green.
Green becomes grow.
Grow becomes vibrant.
Vibrant becomes ripe.
Ripe becomes tassel.
Tassel becomes flower.
Flower becomes pollen.
Pollen becomes airborne.
Airborne becomes silk.
Silk becomes pollination.
Pollination becomes kernels.
Kernels become harvest.
Harvest becomes heat.
Heat becomes steam.
Steam becomes POP!
POP! becomes food.
Food becomes snack.
Snack becomes compost.
Compost becomes earth.
Earth becomes field.
Field becomes fertile.

Interactive Stories

Interactive stories offer the reader a manipulative to move throughout the book in response to the text. The child interacts with the book on both a literary and playful level. My fifth grade students enjoyed making interactive books for the kindergartners each year. Older grades could adapt this form, creating books for primary-age children that highlight concepts within a brief story. Typically, teachers of young children are always appreciative of literature that reinforces concepts such as:

- color words
- number words
- directional phrases (e.g., in the corner, behind the couch, above the bookshelf)
- ordinal numbers
- days of the week
- months of the year
- pronouns
- active verbs
- proper nouns

Designing and producing an interactive book for younger children is a challenge for the older student. Students need first to write simple but engaging stories, with beginnings, middles, and ends.

All of our stories featured a child or animal as the main character. An important concept was included within the context of the story. The authors used as many sight words as possible to keep the readability level accessible to the younger student. Story words like *alligator* were repeated regularly so the younger student would become familiar with them. The older students were asked to print or type their stories (using a bold font) onto 6 to 10 double-page spreads. The students wrote and illustrated these stories on large pieces of oak tag and bound them on the left-hand side with plastic binders so that the finished books could withstand lots of daily use by the readers.

Ask Primary Teachers for Sample Books as Guides

To help your students write a strong story with just a few sentences, ask primary teachers for sample books that are good examples of this. I type these stories out and make transparencies so the children can study the structure, vocabulary, and use of sight words. This seems to help students craft their own stories. A few classroom books that work well for this demonstration are:

- *Baron, Rescue Dog* by Lola Schaefer
- *The Hungry Chickens*—a traditional rhyme illustrated by Kathryn Pond
- *Nothing In The Mailbox* by Carolyn Ford
- *Pumpkin, Pumpkin* by Jeanne Titherington
- *Who Said Moo?* by Harriet Ziefert

Seeing these stories typed and separated according to page breaks helps students see how important each word is.

After students have written a strong story of 50–120 words, it's time to think about design. Ask the librarian for 8 to 12 books that appeal to kindergartners to second graders. Help students notice how large and bold the illustrations are in these books. It helps young readers if the type is positioned in the same place on each page. Another support for young readers is to have a nice match between illustration and text on each page. One sentence per page is usually the maximum.

The Fun Part: Making Books Interactive

Now for the fun part! Each of these books becomes interactive when there is a movable piece that the reader can manipulate throughout the book according to actions in the story. For example, if a book is written about a spider visiting the inside of a house, then a large plastic spider can be attached to the spine of the book with a long string. On each page the reader has the opportunity to place the spider in the spot described in the text. For example, if the spider in the story crawls under the bed, the reader can place the spider under the bed in the picture.

The purpose of the interactive figure is to reinforce understanding of the text and to make reading it fun! Also, it gives the reader an incentive to read thoroughly; if he reads the text correctly, he can find out where to move the object next. The enthusiasm for these books is unbelievable. Kindergarten teachers asked us to create new books that would reinforce the concepts the students were focused on at that time. My fifth graders never got their books back until the end of the year. They delighted in comparing the wear and tear. The more "used" the book looked, the happier they were. Often the primary students used these books as models for books they wanted to create themselves.

One student created a book where a child looked for a missing toy in various parts of the house. The small oak tag figure was attached to the binding with Velcro. If the sentence read, *Billy looked under his bed* then, a Velcro tab was glued onto the picture of the rug beside the bed. When the figure was attached, it looked like Billy was searching beneath the bed.

Story ideas that have been featured in interactive books are:

- a young child buying a different school supply on each day of the week
- missing-pet stories with directional concepts
- how-to or cook books with ordinal numbers
- playground activities for the different months of the year
- getting-dressed books with color words
- ball game stories with proper nouns
- garden stories with number words
- holiday stories
- lost in the woods stories
- zoo stories
- barnyard stories

One student had an oak tag basket tied to the binding. As the reader advanced on each page, she "picked" a different kind of flower to add to the basket. Each flower remained in the basket with the help of Velcro. Interactive books are one way to engage students in thoughtful story writing for a specific audience. It takes patience and planning to make a book that meets the needs of a younger reader. The reward is worth it.

When older writers watch the younger students read and enjoy their books, they have definitely seen the writing process come full-circle.

Historical Fiction

I will admit that historical fiction is one of my favorite genres to explore with students. Each story is set within a specific time period in history. The details of this time period are accurate, but the story itself resonates with a theme that is universal to all readers at all times. There are so many excellent picture books and middle grade novels set in particular historical periods. Here are a few that I have used with success:

Picture Books

- *The Floating House* by Scott Russell Sanders
- *Katie's Trunk* by Ann Turner
- *Nettie's Trip South* by Ann Turner
- *Peppe the Lamplighter* by Elisa Bartone
- *Sweet Clara and the Freedom Quilt* by Deborah Hopkinson

Middle-Grade Novels

- *The Apprenticeship of Lucas Whitaker* by Cynthia DeFelice
- *The Beaded Moccasins: The Story of Mary Campbell* by Lynda Durrant
- *Bull Run* by Paul Fleischman
- *The Clock* by James Lincoln Collier
- *Dakota Spring* by D. Anne Love
- *A Picture of Freedom: The Diary of Clotee, a Slave Girl* by Patricia C. McKissack
- *SOS Titanic* by Eve Bunting

Students need to read a rich assortment of historical fiction before attempting to write their own. After children understand the elements, they are usually quite excited about crafting pieces themselves.

Discuss the Importance of Setting

To begin, I expose the students to three to four picture books. We first enjoy the story for story's sake. Then, we identify the main character, setting, problem, episodes, and resolution. It is always important for the students to see the strong human story inside historical fiction. After this initial discussion, we study the role the setting plays in driving the story. For example, in *Katie's Trunk*, Ann Turner, the author, sets the mood immediately in the book by showing Katie's unrest and orneriness in the first few pages. We get a sense of time from her mama's words: "I should sit you down to sew long seams all day and get the goodness straight inside...."

The author continues and sets the stage even further when she writes: *"These letters your Papa speaks of, that tea they dumped in the harbor." Mama's hand shook. "Tea! In the harbor! Wasting God's good food."* The reader is now getting a sense that Katie and her family are Tories.

We continue to look at the clues the author and illustrator provide to give a sense of time and place. These don't interfere with the story but instead enhance the conflict. That's what good historical fiction does—it uses the setting as a rich nest for story development. In fact, in most historical fiction for children, the character and problem could be placed in another setting, and it would still be a good story. Children need to be shown that most characters in historical fiction do not play a central role in the historical events of the time. Their story or problem is pushed forward by events occurring within that time period. Therefore, it is still important for students to develop a strong character with a genuine problem. However, as they go along, have them note how the problem often arises because of the setting. In other words, the setting often drives the story.

Immerse Students in the Time Period Through Literature

To help students acquire some background for the historical period they want to use in their stories, I ask them to read as much as they can, both fiction and nonfiction, about that particular time. As they learn specific details of one historical setting, they jot down key words on a history wheel. A history wheel is a large circle of oak tag divided into eight pie-shaped sections. Students label the different sections with headings taken from the list on the following page. As they find names, weapons, or political issues of their historical period, they add them to the wheel. I try to provide plenty of independent reading time in the preceding week or two. This allows them to immerse themselves in these books. However, if students have just completed a thorough study of the Civil War, pioneer America in the 1800s, or the Lewis and Clark Expedition in their history class, they will already have a strong understanding of a particular time period and can forego this extra reading.

Students usually select about eight categories of information to research:

- names of people
- names of leaders
- names of important places (cities, rivers, forts, camps, reservations)
- weapons
- articles of clothing
- daily household goods (food, furniture, utensils, room names, house materials, tools, or toys)
- religious or political issues
- transportation and communication vehicles and equipment

These categories vary, depending on the time period and/or the interests of the student.

Of course, students will not use all of this information in their stories, but it gives them a broad range of details. The ones they select will add authenticity to their story.

Develop a Rubric

After the students have completed their history wheels but before they plan, it is time for the teacher and students to draw up a rubric that will guide these stories. Earlier in the year it is advisable to use the same standards for all students; this helps with group critiques and revision, but as the year progresses and the students gain more proficiency in writing, some may want to set their own personal standards for achievement.

Recently I worked with a group of fifth-grade students on writing historical fiction. We collaborated on the development of a rubric for everyone. They decided on these five criteria for their stories. The children tried to tack on about three more, but I asked them to limit themselves to five.

1. **Focus:** entire story is focused on one event

2. **Problem/Conflict:** problem is identified early, there is both internal and external conflict, and the conflict builds throughout the story

3. **"Show, Don't Tell" Language:** active verbs—use of descriptive language—give audience the sense of being in the scene

4. **Story Is Fluid and Clear to the Reader/Listener:** reader/listener understands whole story; it moves smoothly from one scene to another, and all of it carries meaning

5. **Correct Quotation Marks and Spelling:** human and print resources have been used to check accuracy

A fifth grade boy in this class planned and wrote his first piece of historical fiction. Fascinated with a few of the things he had read about Michelangelo, the student decided to research this artist and his time period. Here are the results of his work:

Story Plan by Nathan Hartman, fifth grader

Character: Christopher

Strengths: 1. smart
2. persuasive
3. kind

Faults: too curious, too talkative

Setting: Place: Sistine Chapel

Time: 1508

Problem: Pope and Michelangelo have many arguments and Michelangelo gets discouraged about his work in the Sistine Chapel.

Events: 1. (external)   Pope yells at Michelangelo.
Christopher comes in.

(internal)   Christopher is curious about the disagreement.

2. (external)   Christopher asks Michelangelo what they were saying. Michelangelo says, "I don't do this! I'm a sculptor!"

(internal)   Christopher doesn't want Michelangelo to quit.

3. (external)   Christopher tries to persuade Michelangelo to remain.

(internal)   Christopher wants Michelangelo to stay because he, too, wants to be a painter.

Resolution: Michelangelo starts to quit and Christopher blurts out his feelings. Michelangelo stays.

"For You"
by Nathan Hartman

The City of Rome in the year 1508—buildings, pillars, coliseums, and beautiful sculptures. Busy and happy people are everywhere. But, one place is different. In the Sistine Chapel, which is having a makeover, a famous sculptor and the Pope, who hired him to paint, have many arguments.

"What are you making a mess of now?" the Pope angrily asks.

"Nothing," Michelangelo answers. "I'm just not a painter, I am a sculptor, and you, sir, hired me to paint a ceiling that is going to take a hundred years to complete! Perhaps I quit, how would that be?" Michelangelo asks. Then, a small boy walks through the chapel doors and the Pope storms out.

"What was that all about?" Christopher, a young boy who has befriended Michelangelo, asks.

"Oh, the Pope!"

"Yelling again?" asks Christopher.

"Uh-huh." Michelangelo replies. "I'm not a painter. I am a sculptor and he asks the impossible."

Christopher worries that Michelangelo might quit and says, "I don't think it is impossible. I think you're the greatest painter ever! Look at the beautiful curves and how about the ribbon, how it flows..." Christopher explains.

But Michelangelo interrupts his thoughts. "What do you know about painting, you're only a child," he yells down.

Tears well up in Christopher's eyes and he runs out the doors.

That night when Michelangelo is packing up, he finds some beautiful sketches on the floor.

+ + + + + + +

The next morning, when Christopher comes in the door, Michelangelo is waiting for him with his sketches. "Looks like you're quite an artist," he says.

"Thank you. I want to be an artist, but my mother won't let me. I might as well tear those apart," Christopher says as he points to the sketches.

"No, no. You can be an artist. You just need inspiration..." Michelangelo encourages him. He thinks a while and then says, "When I was little, my mother was very ill, so I stayed with a family of stone masons and they were always there for me when I sculpted. And you need inspiration, too."

He climbs back up the ladder to the platform and says two words, "For you."

A wide smile spreads across Christopher's face.

Historical fiction is a powerful story form. It melds research with human conflict in a way students find compelling. Whether you are a teacher of writing, language arts, English, history, or social studies, this may be an art form that will excite your students about the past and the use of powerful language.

Math Stories

Mathematics is a part of our daily lives. We use estimation and exact math in just about everything we do—from cooking, to measurement, to shopping, to exercise. It is no wonder that some students find working with math concepts a challenging way to add interest to a story.

I generally talk about the math curriculum directly when encouraging students to write stories with a math emphasis. Here are three books among many that I have used as models for students:

⚙ *The Great Pet Sale* by Mick Inkpen
⚙ *Pigs Will Be Pigs* by Amy Axelrod (an entire series of books with math concepts)
⚙ *Sir Cumference and the First Round Table* by Cindy Neuschwander

Again, you want students to develop a good story. The math concept supports the story, not the other way around. I have to admit that, despite my continual encouragement over the years, only a handful of students have written stories with a strong math concept. The one exception to this are the stories students write for younger audiences. Quite a few of their interactive and pop-up books make use of math in an obvious way.

Rubrics, planning, and the writing process all remain the same for this form. If you and the students want to add a standard to your rubric stating, "Use of math concept adds meaning and interest to the story," please do. Remember, a rubric needs to act as a guide in determining the purpose of the story.

Whether published books or student-created ones, "math fiction" tends to have a playful quality to it. The following story was written by a fifth grade boy after he read some of Amy Axelrod's work. This young man has a great sense of humor, and it is quite apparent when you read his story.

"Money Hunt—the Tale of Some Hippos' Night Out"

by Michael Bernard, fifth grader

"Hey, Dad! Can we go see Space Hippos 47 at the theater?"

"Okay, Hungry Hippo, as long as you kids pay for your admission and food," replies Dad.

"Yippie!" shrieks Helga Hippo.

"I need money," moans Hungry.

"I have some!" replies Helga as she races to her room.

"Hey, where'd it go?"

"They looked like chocolate coins," said Hungry with a burp.

"Money Hunt!" yells Helga.

"Let's put our money together," suggests Hungry.

In the piggy bank, Helga found a dollar bill and eight shiny pennies. In the dryer Hungry found a $5.00 bill. Helga found twelve bright quarters in the wishing well. Hungry dug through the coat pockets and found six rusty dimes, five old nickels, and thirteen copper pennies.

Hungry and Helga met together and counted the money.

"Let's go!" exclaimed Helga.

When they got to the theater it was "hippo night" so admission cost them a dollar each.

Once inside they looked at the snacks and saw this sign:

SNACKS

POPCORN	SNACK	BEVERAGE	DOLLAR SPECIAL
Small ....$ .50 Med. ....$ .60 Large ....$ .75 Extra-Large ....$1.00 Super Mega, Ultra Gigantic, Power Size ....$ 3.00	Candy Bar........$ .50 Gum Ball ....$ .05 Hot Dog..........$ .75	Small ....$ .50 Medium ......$ .75 Large ....$ 1.00	Hot Dog, Small Popcorn and Small Pop for $1.00

They each got a special.

Later in the movie as the leader space hippo took over Taiwan, Hungry got a Super Mega Ultra gigantic Power size popcorn, a large Coke, and two hot dogs.

After the movie Helga played a pinball game for $.50 and Hungry bought a gum ball.

"Hey, Dad, can we see Space Hippos 48?" asked Hungry.

"Only if you pay for yourself again."

"How much do we have?" asked Hungry.

"We have (cough, cough, aaaccchhhooo!)" replied Helga. "I need cough medicine."

"Ohhhhh..."

"Money hunt!" yelled Helga.

Michael's story shows us his understanding of character, problem, episodes, and resolution, and he also includes a surprise ending. His writing has a natural cadence that moves the story along at a pleasing rate. The use of math concepts involving adding and subtracting are part of the plot, not the reason for the story. More important—it's fun to read!

Writing stories across the curriculum can be an exciting way to blend knowledge from content areas with the skills of creating engaging stories. As with all story writing, purpose and audience always need to be considered first. These stories should not be written for teacher evaluation only, but for the enjoyment of an authentic audience. Otherwise, we will defeat the true reason for writing—to share a bit of ourselves with the world.

Final Thoughts

Writing is a very personal process. It can be stimulated, encouraged, guided, and appreciated. Writers will find their own words to express their feelings through their chosen forms. Our job is to invite students into a safe, experimental world, where everyone writes and shares the tools they know. Once this is done, let's sit back, read their words, listen to their words, find their meaning, joy, wonder, humor, and compassion and say, "Aaaaaah."

Story Rubric

	EXCELLENT	GOOD	NEEDS WORK
Complete Plan	a brief plan with all story elements	a brief plan with some story elements	incomplete plan
Character	believable and likable	one or the other	neither believable nor likable
Setting	where and when	one or the other	neither where nor when
Problem	a problem the character can solve believable	one or the other	neither
Beginning, Middle, and End	All three can be found in the story.	Two of the three can be found in the story.	One of the three can be found in the story.

Personal Story

	EXCELLENT	GOOD	NEEDS WORK
Focus on One Incident	The writing consistently focuses on one incident from beginning to end.	Most of the writing focuses on one incident.	The writing never fully describes one incident.
Vocabulary	six or more strong, specific words	four or five strong, specific words	three or fewer strong, specific words
Character, Setting, Problem, Resolution	It is easy to identify the characters, setting, problem, and resolution.	The story contains a main character, setting, and problem.	The story contains only one or two story elements.
Varied Sentence Structure	Three or more different sentence structures are used throughout the story.	Two different sentence structures are used.	The same sentence structure is used throughout the story.

Teaching Narrative Writing: The Tools That Work for Every Student

Scholastic Professional Books

Story Map

Title and Author: _____

_____

Main Character: _____

Positive Traits: _____   _____   _____

Flaw, Need, or Fear: _____

Setting: _____

Problem (stated in a complete sentence): _____

_____

Episodes: _____

_____

_____

Solution: _____

Character Growth (How did the main character change?): _____

_____

_____

Scholastic Professional Books

Teaching Narrative Writing: The Tools That Work for Every Student

Name _____ Date _____

Story Plan

Main Character: _____

Strengths: _____

_____

Flaw, Need, or Fear: _____

Setting: **where** _____ **when** _____

Problem (stated in a complete sentence): _____

_____

Episodes: **1.** (external action) _____

(internal action) _____

2. (external action) _____

(internal action) _____

3. (external action) _____

(internal action) _____

Resolution: _____

Character Growth: _____

_____

Teaching Narrative Writing: The Tools That Work for Every Student   Scholastic Professional Books

Dear Parent, Grandparent, or Community Speaker,

Our school invites you into a classroom to speak with children. This year we would like your help in strengthening the skills involved in communicating real-life stories. Students need to see the direct link between oral storytelling and written narrative. We hope you, or someone you know, will volunteer 15 to 20 minutes during the day to present a well-focused story rooted in real events. To enhance the children's language development, each presenter will need to consider the following criteria when selecting a story:

- Is the event or information something appropriate and of interest to this age group?

- What is the purpose in telling this story? Humor? Historical value? Informative? Anecdotal?

- Can I sustain student interest with my presentation style and expression?

- Will my story include a *who* (main character), *when*, *where* (setting), and *what* (three or more events), and an ending (significance or conclusion)?

- How will I begin so that I use my time most effectively in relating the entire story?

Before your visit, the classroom teacher will speak to the students about you and the topic of your presentation. They will brainstorm 3 to 5 questions to ask at the end of your story. They may think of more questions after hearing your story, but the purpose is to teach children to think and ask pertinent questions *focused on the topic*. Please allow an additional five minutes to answer these at the end of your presentation.

Classroom speakers can be scheduled between the dates of _____ and _____. Please contact _____ at this number _____ between the hours of _____ A.M. and _____ P.M. to set up an appointment, or simply return the attached sign-up sheet with a student. Your contribution of a real-life story will be a great addition to the students' language experiences this year.

Thank you for your gift of time.

Sincerely,

Fairy-Tale Story Plan

Once upon a time (or variation thereof)...

Name of hero or heroine _____

Three good traits or special powers: **1.** _____

2. _____ **3.** _____

Setting: **time** (real or fantasy): _____

   place (name and describe): _____

   _____

Problem or Evil to Overcome: _____

_____

Episodes (use of magic is expected):

   1.   ext: _____

       int: _____

   2.   ext: _____

       int. _____

   3.   ext: _____

       int: _____

Any chants or phrases repeated in this story?

_____

Any magical devices or charms?

_____

Resolution: _____

_____

...Lived happily ever after (or variation thereof).

Teaching Narrative Writing: The Tools That Work for Every Student   Scholastic Professional Books

Name _____ Date _____

Tall-Tale Story Plan

Name of bigger than life character: _____

Three good traits or special strengths: **1.** _____

2. _____   **3.** _____

Setting: **time:** _____

         place: (United States) _____

Problem: What phenomenon is the character going to control or create? _____

_____

Is there a special tool, animal, or helper that the character will use? _____

_____

Don't forget the use of hyperbole!!

Episodes:

     1. ext: _____

           int: _____

     2. ext: _____

           int. _____

     3. ext: _____

           int: _____

Resolution (includes extraordinary measures): _____

_____

Celebration: _____

How this story is remembered today: _____

_____

_____

Name _____ Date _____

Historical-Fiction Story Plan

Character: (appropriate name for time period) _____

Three good traits **1.** _____

2. _____ **3.** _____

Flaw, Fear, or Need: _____

Setting: **time:** _____

　　　　　place: _____

Problem (specific to the setting): _____

_____

Episodes:

　　1. ext: _____

　　　　int: _____

　　2. ext: _____

　　　　int. _____

　　3. ext: _____

　　　　int: _____

Resolution: _____

_____

Growth of Character: _____

_____

Teaching Narrative Writing: The Tools That Work for Every Student

Scholastic Professional Books

Short Story Plan

Main Character: _____

Strengths **1.** _____

2. _____ **3.** _____

Flaw, Fear, or Need: _____

Setting: **time:** _____

place: _____

Problem (Stated in a complete sentence): _____

_____

Episodes:

1. ext: _____

int: _____

2. ext: _____

int. _____

3. ext: _____

int: _____

Resolution: _____

_____

Growth of Character: _____

_____

Teaching Narrative Writing: The Tools That Work for Every Student   Scholastic Professional Books

Author's Revision Checklist

☐ Read rough draft out loud to catch missing words or break in meaning.

☐ Do you have a strong beginning with a character, setting, and hint of the problem?

☐ Does your story have action?

☐ Does your main character struggle to solve the problem?

☐ Is the problem believable?

☐ Do the episodes build in conflict?

☐ Does your writing have "voice"?

☐ Does your main character bring about the resolution?

☐ Does your story flow from one event to another?

Author's Editing Checklist

☐ Have you identified misspelled words?

☐ Do you maintain the same tense throughout your story?

☐ Are your sentences easy to read and are they written correctly?

☐ Have you used quotation marks correctly?

☐ Have you used correct punctuation at the end of all your sentences?

☐ Is your title written in capital letters?

Teaching Narrative Writing: The Tools That Work for Every Student   Scholastic Professional Books

Small-Group Critique Session

Ground Rules

Authors need to read their work slowly, loudly, and with expression.

Authors need to accept both positive and critical comments with grace.

Critique members need to be good listeners/readers.

Limit comments to the most important issues of story development.

Critique members need to offer specific comments using a few choice words.

Most important, critique others as you would have them critique you.

Procedure

Groups need to have three or four members for best results.

All members need to come together with rough drafts and pencils or pens.

One member reads his story.

After this first reading, members can ask questions about *purpose* and *audience*.

Members offer positive comments on the story.

If the author has a specific question for the group, he asks it now.

Author reads his story again.

Using a rubric as a guide, members offer suggestions for improvement.

Author may request additional comments.

Author receives all criticism graciously; later, he can determine which to use.

Author or members of the group record critical comments for review.

Group offers final positive comments on the overall story.

Total critique needs to take 6–12 minutes.

Continue the process with another critique group member

Considerations to Assess Story's Meaning:

Overall enjoyment of the story

Tight focus

Meaning is understood—clarity

Purpose and audience

Criteria in the rubric

Beginning, middle, and end

Strong character

Setting

Problem

Episodes with conflict

Resolution

Growth of character

Author's voice

Specific vocabulary

Fluency

Title

Teaching Narrative Writing: The Tools That Work for Every Student   Scholastic Professional Books

Bibliography

Professional Books Cited

Bauer, Marion Dane. *What's Your Story?* New York: Clarion Books, 1992.

Calkins, Lucy. *The Art of Teaching Writing.* Portsmouth, New Hampshire: Heinemann, 1994.

Ueland, Brenda. *If You Want To Write.* Saint Paul, Minnesota: Graywolf Press, 1987.

Fletcher, Ralph. *Live Writing: Breathing Life Into Your Words.* New York: Avon Books, Inc., 1999.

—— *What A Writer Needs.* Portsmouth, New Hampshire: Heinemann, 1993.

—— *A Writer's Notebook.* New York: Avon Books Inc., 1996

Karl, Jean. *How To Write and Sell Children's Picture Books.* Cincinnati, Ohio: Writer's Digest Books, 1994.

Murray, Donald M. *Shoptalk.* Portsmouth, NH: Boynton/Cook Publishers, 1990.

Children's Books Cited

Alexander, Lloyd. *The Fortune-tellers.* New York: Dutton Children's Books, 1992.

Axelrod, Amy. *Pigs Will Be Pigs.* New York: Simon & Schuster, 1994.

Bartone, Elisa. *Peppe the Lamplighter.* New York: Lothrop, Lee & Shepard Books, 1993.

Bauer, Joan. *Backwater.* New York: G.P. Putnam's Sons, 1999.

Baylor, Byrd. *If You Are A Hunter of Fossils.* New York: Aladdin Books, 1980.

Bradby, Marie. *More Than Anything Else.* New York: Orchard Books, 1995.

Bunting, Eve. *Blackwater.* New York: Joanna Cotler Books, 1999.

Bunting, Eve. *SOS Titanic.* San Diego: Harcourt Brace and Company, 1996.

Christiansen, Candace. *The Ice Horse.* New York: Dial Books, 1993

Collier, James Lincoln and Christopher. *The Clock.* New York: Bantam Doubleday Dell Books for Young Readers, 1992.

Crook, Connie Brummel. *Maple Moon.* Toronto, Canada: Stoddart Kids, 1997.

Durrant, Lynda. *The Beaded Moccasins.* New York: Clarion Books, 1998.

DeFelice, Cynthia. *The Apprenticeship of Lucas Whitaker.* New York: Farrar Straus Giroux, 1996.

Fleischman, Paul. *Bull Run.* New York: Scholastic Inc., 1993.

Ford, Carolyn. *Nothing In The Mailbox.* Katonah, New York: Richard C. Owen Publishers, Inc., 1996.

Haddix, Margaret Peterson. *Running Out of Time.* New York: Simon & Schuster, 1995.

Hahn, Mary Downing. *Wait Till Helen Comes.* New York: Avon Books, 1986.

Henkes, Kevin. *The Birthday Room.* New York: Greenwillow Books, 1999.

—— *Lilly's Purple Plastic Purse.* New York: Greenwillow Books, 1996.

Hopkinson, Deborah. *Sweet Clara and the Freedom Quilt.* New York: Alfred A. Knopf, 1993.

Howard, Ellen. *Log Cabin Quilt.* New York: Holiday House, 1996.

The Hungry Chickens. (traditional rhyme) Crystal Lake, IL: Rigby, 1989.

Inkpen, Mick. *The Great Pet Sale*. New York: Orchard Books, 1999.

Keller, Laurie. *The Scrambled States of America*. New York: Henry Holt and Co., 1998.

Littlesugar, Amy. *Jonkonnu*. New York: Philomel Books, 1997.

Love, D. Anne. *Dakota Spring*. New York: Holiday House, 1995.

Lyon, George Ella. *Ada's Pal*. New York: Orchard Books, 1996.

—— *Who Came Down That Road*. New York: Orchard Books, 1992.

MacLachlan, Patricia. *Baby*. New York: Delacorte Press, 1993.

McGuire, Richard. *Night Becomes Day*. New York: Viking, 1994.

McKissack, Patricia C. *A Picture of Freedom: The Diary of Clotee, a Slave Girl*. New York: Scholastic Inc., 1997.

Naylor, Phyllis Reynolds. *Shiloh*. New York: Atheneum, 1991.

Neuschwander, Cindy. *Sir Cumference and the First Round Table*. Watertown, Mass.: Charlesbridge, 1997.

Orr, Katherine. *My Grandpa and the Sea*. Minneapolis, MN: Carolrhoda Books, Inc., 1990.

Paola, Tomie de. *Nana Upstairs and Nana Downstairs*. New York: Puffin Books, 1973.

Paterson, Katherine. *Preacher's Boy*. New York: Clarion, 1999.

Paulsen, Gary. *The Rifle*. New York: Bantam Doubleday Dell Books for Young Readers, 1995.

Pinkwater, Daniel. *I Was A Second Grade Werewolf*. New York: E.P. Dutton, Inc., 1983.

Polacco, Patricia. *Pink and Say*. New York: Philomel Books, 1994.

—— *Thank You, Mr. Falker*. New York: Philomel Books, 1998.

Rinaldi, Ann. *An Acquaintance With Darkness*. San Diego: Harcourt Brace and Company, 1997.

Ryan, Pam Munoz. *Riding Freedom*. New York: Scholastic Press, 1998.

Rylant, Cynthia. *Missing May*. New York: Orchard Books, 1992.

Sanders, Scott Russell. *The Floating House*. New York: MacMillan Books for Young Readers, 1995.

Sayre, April Pulley. *If You Should Hear A Honey Guide*. Boston: Houghton Mifflin Co., 1995.

Schaefer, Lola. *Baron, Rescue Dog*. Katonah, NY: Richard C. Owen Publishers, Inc., 2000

Spinelli, Jerry. *Crash*. New York: Knopf, 1996.

Taylor, Clark. *The House That Crack Built*. San Francisco: Chronicle Books, 1992.

Taylor, Mildred D. *Mississippi Bridge*. New York: Bantam Skylark Books, 1990.

Titherington, Jeanne. *Pumpkin, Pumpkin*. New York: Scholastic Inc., 1986.

Turner, Ann. *Katie's Trunk*. New York: MacMillan Publishing Company, 1992.

Turner, Ann. *Nettie's Trip South*. New York: MacMillan Publishing Company, 1987.

White, E. B. *Charlotte's Web*. New York: HarperCollins Children's Books, 1952.

William, Karen Lynn. *Painted Dreams*. New York: Lothrop, Lee & Shepard Books, 1998.

Wisniewski, David. *Golem*. New York: Clarion Books, 1996.

—— *Rain Player*. New York: Clarion Books, 1991.

Wood, Audrey. *The Napping House*. San Diego: Harcourt Brace Jovanovich, Publishers, 1984.

Woodruff, Elvira. *The Memory Coat*. New York: Scholastic, 1999.

Yolen, Jane. *Owl Moon*. New York: Philomel Books, 1987.

Ziefert, Harriet. *Who Said Moo?* New York: HarperFestival, 1996.

Books On Publishing

Diehn, Gwen. *Making Books That Fly, Fold, Wrap, Hide, Pop up, Twist and Turn.* Asheville, NC: Lark Books, 1998.

Guthrie, Donna and Nancy Bentley and Katy Keck Arnsteen. *The Young Author's Do-It-Yourself Book: How To Write, Illustrate, and Produce Your Own Book.* Brookfield, Conneticut: Millbrook Press, 1994.

Illusory: *Write and Illustrate Your Own Book.* Denver: Chimeric Inc., 1995.

Irvine, Joan and Linda Hendry. *How To Make Super Pop-ups.* New York: Beech Tree Books, 1992.

Johnson, Pauline. *Creative Bookbinding.* New York: Dover Publications, 1990.

Kalman, Bobbie. *How A Book Is Published.* New York: Crabtree Publishing, 1995.

Laplantz, Shereen. *Cover To Cover: Creative Techniques for Making Beautiful Books, Journals, and Albums.* Asheville, NC: Lark Books, 1995.

Pike, Kathy and Jean Mumper. *Books Don't Have To Be Flat! Innovative Ways To Publish Students' Writing In Every Curriculum Area.* New York: Scholastic, 1998.

Sunflower, Cherlyn. *75 Creative Ways To Publish Students' Writing.* New York: Scholastic, 1995.

Walsh, Natalie. *Easy Bookmaking: Thematic Pop-ups, Cards, and Shape Books.* New York: Scholastic, 1996.

Web Sites for Author Interviews and Information

Betsy Byars
http://www.betsyByars.com

Ralph Fletcher
http://www.ralphfletcher.com

Jean Craighead George
http://www.jeancraigheadgeorge.com

Internet Public Library
http://www.ipl.org/youth/AskAuthor/Avi.htl

Katharine Paterson
http://www.terabithia.com

Patricia Polacco Web Page
http://www.patriciapolacco.com

Pam Munoz Ryan
http://www.pammunozryan.com

The Scoop—Author Interviews
http://www.friend.ly.net/scoop/interviews/index.html

Aaron Shepard's Young Author Page
http://www.aaronshep.com/youngauthor

Jerry Spinelli
http://www.carr.lib.md.us/authco/spinelli-j.htm

David Wisniewski
http://www.eduplace.com/rdg/author/wisniewski/index.html